FAMILYHOOD

ALSO BY
PAUL REISER

Couplehood
Babyhood

PAUL REISER

FAMILYHOOD

HYPERION

NEW YORK

Library of Congress Cataloging-in-Publication Data
has been applied for.

ISBN: 978-1-4013-2432-2

Book Design by Karen Minster

Hyperion books are available for special promotions and
premiums. For details contact the HarperCollins
Special Markets Department in the New York
office at 212-207-7528, fax 212-207-7222,
or email spsales@harpercollins.com.

FIRST EDITION

10   9   8   7   6   5   4   3   2   1

THIS LABEL APPLIES TO TEXT STOCK

We try to produce the most beautiful books possible, and
we are also extremely concerned about the impact of our
manufacturing process on the forests of the world and the
environment as a whole. Accordingly, we've made sure
that all of the paper we use has been certified as coming
from forests that are managed, to ensure the protection of
the people and wildlife dependent upon them.

To Paula, Ezra, and Leon

With all the love there could possibly be

CONTENTS

PREFACE

WHEN THEY WERE WELL INTO THEIR SIXTIES, MY PARENTS renewed friendships with some of their old friends. These were close friends from their school days, friends from old neighborhoods—good friends that I had no recollection of ever having met growing up. Where had these people been? I wondered. If they were such good friends, how come I never heard of them?

My parents' simple explanation was that they had all drifted apart when they were busy raising their families, but now that the kids were older, they had picked up the friendships again.

This was fascinating to me. First of all, the drifting apart. It's not like any of them moved to the North Pole; they were all pretty close by, but they somehow managed to never see each other.

Secondly—I didn't know you could do that with friendships; put them on hold for fifteen, twenty, twenty-five years, and then just start right up again.

And I had no idea that having kids and doing simple day-to-day stuff was so all-encompassing that it could necessitate putting entire friendships—*good* friendships—on hold.

WELL, THAT'S KIND OF HOW I FEEL about this book. I wrote two books before this; the first one about meeting and marrying my beautiful wife, the second one about the journey before, during, and after having a baby.

That was fifteen years ago. In that time, our infant firstborn became fifteen, his brother—now ten—joined the team, and a gazillion day-to-day things had to be dealt with: there were the countless hectic meals where nobody sits down at the same time, frantic rushes to start school reports that should have been finished weeks earlier, knees that needed bandaging and glasses that needed finding—even though they were "right there" five minutes ago—and more arguments than you can imagine about why long pants were in order even though, yes, shorts are more comfortable. My point is—things got busy around here.

Along the way, there were certainly plenty of things that occurred to me, observations I might have written down for, say, a book about having kids, but I couldn't because I was too busy (and exhausted by) having those very same kids.

I'd like to say that somehow the clouds have lifted a bit and there seems to be a moment of relative quiet. In truth, things are only going faster. Life is, if anything, crazier than before.

But I realize that my boys are probably closer in time to when they'll leave our house than the time we first brought them home. Whatever I may feel about time, it's going ahead. And I don't want to wait twenty-five years to reconnect with my friends. And with you. (By the way—when I say "you," it's not like I'm being flip, using the figurative, cumulative "you." I actually mean specifically *you*.)

SO WHAT FOLLOWS are some thoughts I've had, some observations I've made, some hopes I humbly put out there, because I've discovered that while yes, my family is my family, unique and quirky, *everyone's* family is unique and quirky, and everyone's family is the same. More or less.

I would also add that seeing as how, at this rate, I likely won't write another book till deep into my nineties, I would suggest: if there are any questions, ask them now, because by that point I may not be making any sense at all.

P.R.
Los Angeles, 2011

FAMILYHOOD

Family

I T'S A FUNNY WORD—*FAMILY*. IT CAN MEAN A LOT OF DIF-ferent things, depending how you use it in a sentence.

There's the smile-drenched "Yeah—going to have a nice relaxing weekend, just me and the *family*." Versus the clench-jawed "Uch—I got the whole *family* coming in for a week! It's going to be brutal!" Same word—and in this case—same *family*. But very different meaning.

We all hold on to some image of the family we *want*, based one way or another on the family we *had*. Lots of people are thrilled about the families they came from, others couldn't get away fast enough. Most people fall into that vast middle ground: great affection mixed with a few ideas for improvement. A couple of things they wish could have perhaps been done differently.

That's where starting your own *new* family comes in handy. You get to start from scratch and get it right.

I don't know about you, but growing up, I kept an actual list, a lengthy running tally called "Things I'm Not So Crazy About in My Family." I kept it in my pocket (and in the forefront of my brain) at all times, for the express purpose of being better prepared when the time came to raise a family of my own.

Years later, that time came—and I was ready. *This*, I said to myself with unwavering confidence, will be the ideal family! How could it not? I mean, I know exactly how I want a family to be now,

I've married a woman with a perfectly compatible blueprint in mind, we're equally determined to get everything right . . . Yesiree, this is going to be it!

Ah . . . there's such *promise* at the beginning, isn't there?

Well, as with *any* attempt to start society over from scratch, it doesn't always work out as planned. You pick the perfect deserted island, you bring in fresh, pristine people, you set it up just *so*, and before you know it the constituents of the New World are squabbling and shoving their way through their overcrowded, polluted, crime-ridden paradise exactly like last time. It's just the way it goes.

WITH BUILDING A FAMILY, what remains unknown is specifically *how* you'll fall short of your goals. In exactly what *new* ways you'll get it wrong. That's the mystery. That's the sport to the whole thing.

Sometimes it's simply that the paradigms have shifted. My children and I grew up in different millennia, in different parts of the country, at different points in history. So many variables have changed.

As a kid, I grew up with a mom and dad, three sisters, no dog (though that's all I really wanted), and periodically, some fish. As a grownup, I have a wife, two boys, a dog, and *no* fish. The rules are necessarily different. Boys, for example, play differently. They fight differently. They certainly smell different.

So, what I've brought with me from my original family does not necessarily apply to this *new* family.

I grew up on the East Coast, my children are growing up in Southern California. They don't *have* to take a jacket every day; it's seventy-five degrees out. But I'm still thinking of the wrong childhood; on this day in October in *my* childhood, it would have been cold out. Here it's not, but I haven't adjusted properly. I continue to run after them in the streets with sweatshirts yelling, "Do you not see what month it is?" (The psychological damage to my children has not yet been fully assessed.)

Sometimes it's something new that takes you down; something you couldn't have known about. It turns out, for example, I've underestimated the significance of video game-playing skills. I've never had any particular dexterity with my opposing thumbs, or hand-eye coordination or, for that matter, any real interest. We didn't have these games when I was a kid, so I couldn't have anticipated that this particular shortcoming would lead to my own kids growing up nursing the pain of their father's glaring absence from this sphere of their lives. Who knew?

But even the areas of concern I *did* see coming, the very things I sought to adjust from my own childhood, may end up "corrected" but not necessarily any better.

Example: Growing up, if I wished for anything it was perhaps that my dad—who worked nobly and tirelessly around the clock—would perhaps work a little less and hang around the house a little more. So I grew up determined to do it differently with my own family.

As best as I've been able, I've endeavored to always put work second and make it my priority to be home and "just be there" for my kids. Result? My kids wouldn't mind if I were actually "there" a little less. I've heard the prayers: "Oh, Lord, could you maybe get my dad out of the house once in a while, and if possible, could he go away for a couple of days sometime? We're talking two, three days tops. Really, we'll be fine. Leave Mom here, though."

I made notes not just about kid-raising; I also jotted down a few things about marriage—or at least *my parents'* marriage, which was, after all, my only real point of reference. I had some very concrete ideas about what I wanted to change, and what I wanted to keep; what I thought worked and *didn't* work—as I understood it from my kid's-height view.

Definitely saw a lot of love and a lot of commitment. Keep. Selfless devotion and sacrifice for their children. Keep.

But I also remember wishing my father would have *noticed* my mother a bit more. Been perhaps a tad more demonstrative. Or tangibly appreciative. Which is not to say he wasn't appreciative; I'm sure he was. Just not so's you'd notice.

And, shrewdly working the other side of the aisle, I simultaneously and actively wished my mother would notice a little bit *less* that my father didn't seem to notice her so much.

What I took away from the experience, though, was a commitment to be different when *I* had a family. I was determined to be unbelievably and demonstratively appreciative of *my* wife. Which has paid off handsomely—with the exception of the countless *thousands* of times my wife has nonetheless felt forlornly underappreciated.

I clocked the rules of engagement in my house growing up; the way we communicated with each other as a family. In a word, I think it's safe to say that *clarity* was not our strong suit. Nothing said was exactly what you wanted to say, and what you were aching to say was, regretfully, almost always left unsaid. Almost *encouraged* to remain unsaid. My remedy? Go the other way. In my "new and improved" family, I leave no sentiment unexpressed, no feeling unshared, no fleeting thought unspoken. Good, right? Not really.

"Dad, dial it down, wouldya? That's just too much information."

"Really? But I thought you'd want to—"

"No. We're kids. We don't need to hear *everything*."

Do you see the problem here? There's virtually *no* way to win.

Striving to make your new family different from your first family is no easy task. And, I've come to realize, making it your life's work to be different than your parents is not only hard to do, it's a dumb idea. Not everything we found fault with was necessarily wrong; we were right, for example, to resent, as kids, being told when to go to bed. We'd be equally *wrong*, as parents, to let our kids stay up all night. To throw out all the tools of parenting just because your parents used them would be like making yourself speak English without using ten letters of the alphabet; it's hard to do, very limiting, and . . . makes it impossible for foreigners to understand you over the phone. (Which, while not germane to my point about parenting, I felt was worth mentioning.)

I KNOW MY WIFE AND I will raise our kids to the best of our ability. Undoubtedly, our kids will have their own counterbalances in place, and swing back the other way with their own families, messing up their kids in the exact opposite direction. *Their* kids will hear nothing direct or emotional from *their* fathers, resent them for never being home, and wonder why, when they *were* home, they never told the kids to take a jacket when it's cold out.

And so the cycles will repeat, on and on through time, until the earth is pulled so close to the sun that I'm guessing nobody's going to need a jacket anyway.

Roll, Pitch, and Yaw

BEFORE I WAS A FATHER, I SORT OF IMAGINED THE JOB as being the captain of a ship; you carefully steer your kids through life's icebergs and storms so that they can sail forth through life's many exciting adventures.

Not sure why my brain took me to the nautical. Never captained a ship in my life. I once tried to take the boys kayaking and pulled something in my shoulder that has never been quite the same since. I think I just liked the *image* of being a ship captain: strong and stoic, meeting every emergency with calm, maintaining order among the crew, who would come to love my quiet, controlled leadership. (And from what I understand from pirate movies, you get better food and a niftier hat.)

All in all, fathering—like captaining—seemed to be an exciting journey. Challenging, but certainly doable. Just keep a steady hand on the wheel, and make sure nobody goes off course.

Turns out, children are not so easy to steer.

My younger son was having a problem with his homework. No subject in particular; he just doesn't like doing homework. He's incredibly bright and, if he so elected, could finish any given night's work in a matter of minutes. But he is so vehemently against the very *idea* of homework that he waits till the very possible last minute, then does it so grudgingly and recklessly that it's really something to behold.

As a father, I felt it was my job to steer him toward approaching homework with a bit more care and concern. Also, I didn't want to have a mutiny—which, as I understand it, is the main thing you want to avoid when you're a sea captain. (Particularly when the mutineer is only forty-eight inches tall.)

My son, however, was not particularly interested in being steered. It wasn't exactly a mutiny, but my little crewmember was not embracing my steering. The homework did not get any better.

Fortunately, I have a co-captain: my wife. *Un*fortunately, she had no idea what to do either. No amount of helpful, gentle encouragement from either of us seemed to do the trick. Homework continued to come in late, ketchup-stained, or illegible. I pointed out that his "5" could easily be read as a "3," and the odd squiggle he intended to be a "7" is also, ironically, the Chinese character symbol for "impale" or "to have impaled." My son contended that everyone but me would know what these figures were just fine.

He also had a tendency to illustrate the borders of his homework with a very impressive series of sketches—generally of some military confrontation between giant robots and stick figure gladiators. All very creative—just not necessarily relevant to the work. Or appropriate. To *anything*.

Somehow my precious offspring wasn't quite grasping the concept of what was at stake here.

"This is *homework*," I declared, as if the paper we were holding were some unearthed, holy document. Some sacred text.

His rebuttal: "So?"

"So, homework is a *very big thing*," I said.

"No, it's not," he countered. "It's the same stuff we do in school, and I already did it in school, and I know the answers, so why do we have to go through it again at home?"

Clearly a mutiny was a-brewing. I had to go deeper; push the envelope of my inspirational skills. I explained why homework was so important to his future as a student. And as a man. It wasn't just about getting the answers right, I clarified for him. It was about developing disciplines, setting and achieving goals, meeting expectations—and maybe once in a while even trying to *exceed* expectations. (Though that didn't seem likely. The idea of this guy ever voluntarily doing one ounce more than the barest minimum required was a laughable dream I had all but surrendered years earlier.)

I tried to impress upon him that more than anything, doing his best—at homework or at *anything*—was a matter of self-respect, and respect for others.

No takers. I dug deeper still. I explained how *failing* to do homework properly inevitably leads to a downward school career spiral, diminished earning capacity as an adult, the likelihood of homelessness, and quite possibly a life in crime, which, if pursued without basic math and grammatical skills, could only end in imprisonment or death. I let him know that by failing to do his homework, he wasn't just letting down his mom and dad (and grandmothers, who were kept apprised of the continuing drama), but also his big brother, and—I hated to say it—the nation as a whole; American kids are struggling so badly in school now that it's very likely that elementary school homework may soon be sent to kids in India—who will do it faster, neater, more accurately, and—I'm willing to bet—cheaper. Finally, as the great-grandson of immigrants, he was—as an American—failing to hold up his end of the Social Contract.

Something in there got to him. He apparently hadn't thought of it like that.

Overnight, the homework improved dramatically. He started taking it seriously. He *wanted* to do well, and was firmly committed to never letting his standards drop again.

I was so happy, I didn't notice that in the process, he had also acquired a slight nervous tic and wasn't sleeping very well.

"Why is he so anxious all of a sudden?" my co-captain wife asked.

I shrugged. "No idea. But did you see his math homework? He actually did the extra credit part!" I couldn't help but gloat a little bit. "I think the talk he and I had really helped."

"Did you actually tell him we'd be thrown out of the country if his homework didn't improve?"

"Huh?"

"He said that you said—"

"No, no. Well . . . not exactly in those words."

Apparently I had *over*corrected.

The next night, I went into his room and there was the same kid, hard at work, at his desk—whereas before, his customary work mode had him sprawled across his bed in a sea of scattered Lego pieces and corn chips. This time, it was well past his bedtime as he sat fretting over some long division problems and the fact that he hadn't yet studied for a vocabulary test.

"It's okay," I told him, as calmly and reassuringly as I could. "You can finish in the morning."

"No, I *can't*! I need to finish it now, because—"

"Listen to me. You did the best you could tonight and—"

"But I didn't finish my—"

"Shh, shhh. C'mon. Let's get some sleep. Tomorrow is a new day."

"But—"

I cupped his beautiful, agitated little face in my hands and said, "It's just homework."

A quiet descended. He was a bit relieved, but more than that, confused. As he looked at me through very puzzled, slightly squinted eyes, I could see him recalibrating everything he had come to understand thus far in life, specifically anything he'd ever heard from me.

While he said nothing, it was clear to me he was thinking, "You . . . you really don't know what you're doing, do you?"

In a word: not really.

STEERING, IT TURNS OUT, is not so easy. Too much in either direction is no good. And if you steer too briskly, people can fall overboard.

I put my son to bed, both of us banking on the hope that the light of day would make the world right.

But that brief exchange caused me to realize just how much of what parents tell their children—if not *all* of what we tell our children—is based on remarkably inexact science. We may have a good sense of what's right and what's wrong, what's beneficial and what's detrimental, but when pressed to act upon those instincts, we are *so* just making it up. And we make it up all day long; a steady bombardment of well-intentioned contradiction.

"Come on, why don't you go out and get some fresh air" is followed by "Come on in—you're getting too much sun."

"Play with your brother" ends up with "Why don't you give your brother a little time to himself?"

"No more pretzels—have some fruit" leads to "Why would you eat *seven* bananas?"

"When you meet people, look them in the eye and say 'Hello'" is hard to do when you've already been instructed "Do not talk to strangers."

I'm actually amazed that my children aren't perpetually dizzy.

"Read a book" and "Put the book away and go to sleep."

"If you're not sure, just ask" vs. "Come on—you can figure it out for yourself."

The suggestions are not only contradictory, but often arbitrary.

"Why don't you give that man on the corner this dollar—he's hungry" is followed with an urgent "No, no, sweetie, not your *whole piggy bank*. Just . . . a little."

"Oh. How much do I give?"

"Um, I don't know, actually. Okay—that's fine. We'll go get you another piggy bank."

(When my older guy was about eight, he saw a guy standing on a corner and sweetly handed him five dollars. As we walked away, I gently explained that while I loved his spirit of generosity, this particular fellow wasn't actually homeless—he was waiting for a bus.)

THERE IS NO END to the pushing and pulling, trying to get the balance just right. And when you have more than one kid, you not only have that many more people to balance individually, but you have to maintain the balance *between* them too.

At its simplest, there's the exhausting attempt to keep things equal.

"Why does he get fifteen minutes more of TV?"

"Because you had more yesterday."

Or "How come he gets to pick where we're going for supper?"

"Because you picked last time, now *this* time *he* picks. Next time, *neither* of you picks."

But that's a walk in the park compared to the much trickier judgment calls and interminable calculations we make to push (or pull) each of them in the particular areas we believe they need to be pushed. Or pulled.

I have one kid who needs to take things more seriously; the other could afford to lighten up a tad. I have one who is innately anxious, one absurdly reckless. One child is a "hugger," the other not so much. My younger son—though loving and affectionate— has to be practically paid off (cash only) to indulge a hug from his grandmothers. By contrast, my older son will hug anyone not currently behind bars. Neither is right, neither is wrong; both just need a little adjusting. But it's the specifics where you get tripped up; it's like cooking from a recipe that's been destroyed at the margins—you know what goes into the cake, but they don't tell you *how much* or *when* it's supposed to be dropped in.

Most frightening of all is that *nobody* has the answers for you. You're the captain. And the crew is looking a little nauseous.

I HAVE A FRIEND who flies airplanes. Not the little ones with the remote control box that you take to the park and try not to fly into people's dogs. I'm talking about *real* planes. With landing wheels and wings and cup holders; the kind of plane that could take you from one state to another. And also crash upon takeoff.

I had a hard time understanding why this otherwise responsible and conservative guy with a lovely wife and kids would elect to take on an activity that involves potentially falling from the sky and hurtling to a certain death.

"It's relaxing," he told me.

"Really," I said, unconvinced. "The crashing part doesn't bother you?"

"You have to understand," he said, patiently. (I was obviously not the first one in his life to question this particular choice.) "The plane doesn't *want* to crash."

"Maybe," I said. "The plane also probably doesn't want to go to Bridgeport for the weekend, but it goes. The plane doesn't always get a say in the matter."

"But it does. Because"—and here he paused again for dramatic purposes, practically willing me to embrace this—"the plane *wants* to fly."

He then launched into a complicated dissertation on the laws of physics and momentum. Once the plane gets up in the air, he explained, it *wants* to stay up in the air. In fact, what with energy and thrust and so forth, the plane almost always *will* stay up in the air, flying. So long as the engines don't stop working and the wings stay on, crashing is almost impossible.

"But it happens," I pointed out, fairly unnecessarily.

"Sure," he said. "But usually because of things out of our control. So I just focus on what I *can* control: roll, pitch, and yaw."

I thought that was perhaps the name of the legal firm handling his estate. "Eddie Roll, Markus Pitch, and Simon Yaw—Making Things Right Since 1984."

Turns out, no. Roll, pitch, and yaw are, in fact, aviation terms. As best I could understand it, if you imagine a plane flying through the air, there are three imaginary axes: front-to-back, side-to-side, and up-and-down. These are the areas you want to concern yourself with when piloting.

"Roll" is the way the wings dip up or down, "pitch" is the way the nose goes up or down, and "yaw" is the way the nose goes left and right. (This, by the way, is one reason I myself will never fly a plane; what I just explained to you there is the upper limit of what my brain can digest.)

But basically, my pilot friend explained, if you manage the pitch and the roll and the yaw—countering sudden changes by rooting yourself as best you can back to center—you're pretty much home free.

"And raising kids," he told me, "is a lot like flying."

I was a bit miffed upon hearing this last bit.

"Are you sure it's not like being the captain of a boat?" I asked, irritated that my brilliant analogy had to now be chucked. "Because I had the whole 'boat thing' worked out pretty solidly."

"No, it's more like flying," he assured me. "Because flying has that extra third dimension. Raising kids is definitely more like flying a plane."

SO FORGET ABOUT the boat captain thing. I was wrong; kids are like a plane. And you're like the pilot, but only a little. In truth, the kid takes off and flies less because of what you do and more because of how the kid is designed. Once they're up, they're going to be buffeted and pushed around plenty by bad weather and strong winds and angry turbulence. No way to avoid it. As the pilot, you make your adjustments. That's your job. Do it as best you see fit.

But take comfort knowing that in the end, they'll fly. Because they *want* to fly.

P.S. ANYONE INTERESTED in a perfectly good "boat captain" analogy? Only used once. Call if interested.

Like a
Half Hour

—◦◦◦—

M Y WIFE AND I HAVE ESTABLISHED SOME IRONCLAD rules and traditions that serve to keep our family strong, connected, and grounded:

- We always have dinner together as a family. (Except for those nights when we don't—which is most nights. One of us is working late, or the kids are a bit too wild, and we're unable to pull it off . . . something usually gets in the way.)
- We always go over the kids' homework with them before they pack it away. (Except for the days we don't—which is most days—because the kids were fooling around too much and didn't finish the homework, or it was too hard and neither of us could explain it to them, or we decided that ultimately it's not that important, they can do it tomorrow.)
- We never raise our voices or speak to another member of the family out of anger. (Except for the times we do—which is often enough because . . . well, just *because*. We're a family; who are we gonna yell at—strangers?)

(It should be noted that we continue to keep all these seldom-met objectives on the books because it's important to have goals. Like world peace; it may not happen, but how do you not try?)

The one practice we do insist upon and stick to no matter what (except for those nights when we *don't*—which is almost every night) is: we sit down together—the two of us—and just *connect*.

This may seem a mighty meager aspiration—to simply talk to the person with whom you have committed to share your life—but I assure you it is not. It is, in fact, almost impossible. (If you think otherwise, you either have no children currently living at home or are so supremely organized that, frankly, we might not be able to be friends.)

First of all, the goal itself is multi-pronged. There are actually *two* distinct categories of things upon which we aim to "connect."

There's the simpler—though more exhausting—recounting and updating of all matters of business currently at hand.

"The guy came to fix the dishwasher but he didn't have the part—he's rescheduling for next week."

"You have to pick up the kids at school tomorrow because my eleven o'clock meeting got pushed to two-thirty."

"You forgot to sign that thing for the insurance thing . . ."

"Did we respond to your cousin Ellen's daughter's thing? Because they left a very hostile voice message, you have to listen—you can't believe it."

You know—the fun stuff.

Then of course there's the more intimate kind of catching up. "How *are* you?"—and all the derivations thereof. More important matters, to be sure. But invariably, these get relegated to second position, as the more pressing mundane issues—"the dog threw up again"—take precedence.

What happens—virtually every night—is that as the time approaches to execute this mutually agreed upon covenant to put the world aside and connect with each other, the two parties involved are too darn tired. And if not literally exhausted, certainly so up to our ears in minutiae and momentum after a full day's marathon of work, kids, and the rest of the world, that the very last thing either of us wants to do at that moment is *talk*. To each other, or to anybody. And we *certainly* don't need to talk about all the things that we failed to get done that day and need to start scheduling for the next day.

So we grant ourselves a buffer zone. A little "transition time." A bridge between "work world" and "home world." Traditionally, this would have been accomplished with a stop off after work at the "corner tavern" for "a few cold ones." Well, we don't so much *have* a corner tavern, and if we do, I can tell you with confidence we've never stopped off, and even at home, we're not generally big proponents of "a few cold ones."

What we do instead is take a moment and go our separate ways.

And *that,* my friends, is how the wife and I water the garden of our love: we designate a chunk of time every night, first chance we get, and proceed to deliberately and thoroughly ignore each other's each and every need.

Again, this is done for the communal good; the orchestrated "push away" is only so that, later, we'll be that much more ready to intimately connect. We will be refreshed and replenished, and ready to engage.

Except it never works out.

And not for lack of effort, or sincere intentions. We earnestly plot this out every night. First, we calculate what we each have to do and negotiate a "meet up" time.

"I just have to check my emails," I'll say.

"Perfect—I just need to return two phone calls and look over some papers," my wife will counter.

"So . . . what do you think? Like . . . *a half hour*?"

"Perfect," she says. "Meet you upstairs in half an hour."

And this always, *always* works.

Unless one of us goes online. Then it all goes terribly wrong. If either of us sits at a computer, the enormous Black Hole of emails and online distraction swallows us up whole, and we never see each other again.

THE IRONY IS that the whole point of email and the reach of the Web was to make our lives better, communicating easier. Sadly, it has made it *so* easy that there's no real incentive to ever stop.

Before emails were invented, "getting back to people" involved checking your answering machine to see who called and either calling them back or, more likely, making a note to call them tomorrow. That was it. You didn't go looking for *more* people to get back to.

But with emails, with the entirety of humanity an equal and simple click away, the pull is too great, and we all succumb.

So what used to be "I'm going to just call Larry back" has now become "I'm going to just check and see if *everyone I've ever met* is trying to reach me, and if they are, I will respond, then wait for their response to my response, and while I'm waiting, I'm going to go see if any of the little video clips that kid in the office sent me are funny and, if they are—or even if they're not—just pop a quick response saying why I thought it was funny—or *not* funny—and then maybe send it to some other friends who might find it funny, and while I wait to hear back from them if they thought it was funny too, I just need to see what's happening around the world in terms of news and weather, and, while I'm at it, check out scores of sports

I don't even necessarily follow, and then *possibly*—I might not do this, but I *might*—take a quick look at the thing that pops up offering to show what the various cheerleaders for those teams look like, and—you know what?—maybe scroll through some images of cheerleaders from *all* the various professional sports franchises— just to compare and contrast, and then—hey, look at that—Larry already got back to me. I'm going to send him that video clip too—I bet *he'll* think it's funny—and while he's looking that over, I'm— just for a second—going to see what items are currently available for purchase around the globe—both in stores and also in people's personal attics—maybe even put a bid on a—hey, look at that— this guy is selling a *Camaro* for $15—something must not be right. I bet that kid Billy from eleventh grade would know about that— man, that guy knew about *Camaros*. Wonder what ever happened to Billy . . . I'm going to search around . . . Wow—he lives in Ceylon? How did that happen? I'm going to email him and . . . I'm going to check out my whole graduating class, see what they're up to . . . Wow . . . I can't believe *she* died, she was so pretty. I wonder if Billy knows she died . . . I'm going to ask him . . . I'm going to see who else died and then write to everyone from school who would have known them and say, 'Can you believe it?' and thereby initiate a never-ending correspondence with *those* people. So . . . I'll be up in like . . . I don't know . . . a half hour?"

IT JUST DOESN'T seem to happen.

When I finally do push away from my desk, a good two or three hours later, I stumble upstairs, dazed and drained, to find my beloved either sound asleep with her iPad on her face, or sitting up, equally zombied—her hair sticking up like from a cartoon explosion—little, tiny birds circling and chirping around her head. A brilliant woman now incapable of speech—certainly unable to *connect, share,* or *plan* out the week for her family. If I strain, I can make out her pathetic mumblings. "I don't know what happened." Or maybe a pleading "Can we please talk tomorrow? Must, go, sleep."

And then she's out like a light, followed instantly by me collapsing next to her, my very last conscious thought of the day being "Must throw out computer."

FORTUNATELY, we're a family of discipline and rules, so tomorrow we get to do this again.

Leave a Tender
Moment Alone

—◆—

I T'S REMARKABLE, REALLY, HOW MANY THINGS I CAN DO that irritate my children. Without even trying that hard.

My forte seems to be those *special* moments. The kind that mean the most, that give your life meaning. You know—the ones you want to treasure forever.

Birthdays, for example, or holidays, when everyone is gathered to celebrate happy times that you're going to want to remember forever, with, say, the aid of a nice photograph. Or *two* photos, just in case. Because you're going to hate yourself if you don't get the shot right. It's not like you're ever going to get another chance; this is a special moment. And because it *is* special, there are likely to be other guests in your house. Maybe even relatives from out of town. Loved ones who don't get here that often, who may not be with us that much longer, for example. All the more reason you'd be crazy not to take the extra nanosecond required to maybe get a *third* shot. From a different angle.

"DAD!!!!" MY BOYS WHINE in that special way they have. (Who exactly invented that, by the way—the Petulant Child Eye Roll? Any idea? Because I'd like to talk to them and, at the very least, make sure they're not working on anything new. Like an Abrasively Dismissive Ear Tug. Or a Huffy Irritable Mouth Pucker with Optional

Sucking Noise. The kids seem to be doing fine with just the Eye Roll.)

I can, admittedly, be a little overreaching in orchestrating these photo ops.

"Hey," I cheerily suggest. "Why don't we all just get up and go into the living room where the light is better?"

"No! Forget it," come the cries of resistance.

"Okay," I counter. "Why don't we just open up the curtains and maybe stand near the—"

"Daaaaad!"

At this point my wife will generally suggest—as gently as she can—that the moment has perhaps sailed away, and it might be best to cut our losses and move on. I try to salvage at least one shot—albeit not in the optimum setting.

"Okay, just stand right there—this will only take a second. And I promise you guys: one day you'll be glad you have this."

"No we won't!" the boys say in unison. (It's nice to see how they can work together when they want to.) I take the picture.

"Finally!" the boys say. They're relieved. Now they can get back to having fun. Almost.

"Wait, wait," I call after them. "I want to get it on video too."

"Aww, Dad! Why? You just took pictures."

"I know, but—"

"Can't you just scroll through the pictures really fast so it looks like a movie?"

"First of all," I feel obliged to mention, "that's very funny. And second of all, no. They didn't come out that great. You were moving. Now, go stand next to Grandma and do . . . something video-worthy. Hug her. Smile. Wave."

"Do we have to?"

"Yes."

So with literally no joy or love in their heart, they drag their feet over to the couch and sit next to Grandma, and proceed to be entirely still.

"Do something," I tell them.

"Like what?" they ask.

"I don't care. Just say something."

"What should we say?"

"Whatever you want. Maybe you could talk about what you think your life will be like living on your own starting tomorrow."

The subtlety lands. They grudgingly mug and goof around and say funny things for the camera.

"There you go," I say, happy to have this production finally up and running. I check the camera viewer.

"Oh, nuts," I blurt out.

"What?"

"The memory card is full. Let me just—"

"Daaaad!!!"

"Hold on. Hold on—I just have to clear some of this old stuff from the chip. Just keeping doing what you're doing—having fun, enjoying the moment."

"We're not enjoying anything!" they clarify.

"It's okay, let them go," Grandma graciously suggests. "We'll do it another time."

"No, no—I'm almost ready, here—oops—that's the wrong button."

"Daaddd!"

Truth be told, I am not particularly skilled or competent with technological things in the first place. Add to that the pressure of single-handedly trying to orchestrate a moment that everyone else present is actively resisting, and my performance suffers. I consistently do every wrong thing that can be done. I shoot with batteries that are near empty, memory cards that are near full, I leave the lens cap on, I'm recording when I think I'm not, or I'm *not* recording when I think I *am*. Way more often than you'd think possible, I unwittingly have some button pressed that makes everything look like I'm either shooting from the center of a fire or, conversely, like I'm looking through night vision goggles in a bleak desert storm and the only image discernible is a dimly lit three-inch circle in the middle of the screen—usually of some indeterminate stomach.

And while it's possible I'm imagining this, it seems to me that the moments most frequently lost to human error are exactly the ones you'd most want to have. The ones least likely to ever repeat. Those are the ones I've almost never gotten. On the other hand, looking out a plane window and shooting into the sun—*that* I've never missed. If that's something you enjoy seeing, by the way, you've got to come over. I have hours on end of nothing but airport runways barely visible behind blinding sun flares.

There may be a perfectly valid explanation for this, though. Some larger law of the universe may in fact be at play. I believe it's entirely possible that the Higher Powers don't actually want you to record for posterity the most magical of moments. By not having the image tangibly in hand, they've decided, you're forced instead to remember more clearly, investing yourself more deeply in that golden moment. This way the memory can only grow in recollected detail and mythological import, whereas the actual earthly footage would have likely only disappointed. (Even if this is not the case— which might be the case—I'm going to choose to believe it anyway. It sure beats accepting that I am as untalented in this arena as I appear, and that I'm doomed to a life of pained apologies and disappointed loved ones.)

I just want to have a nice keepsake that we can treasure later on. Is that too much to ask?

The irony is that my boys love looking at old photos and always wish we had taken more. What they don't like is the intrusion necessary to get them.

Surely they are not the first to feel this way; they are part of a long-standing tradition of annoyed and put-upon artistic subjects. I'm guessing that had Da Vinci actually been alive to paint *The Last Supper* at the time that it really was the last supper, the Apostles would've been very irritated with him.

"Uh . . . Peter? Could you hold the goblet up a bit and maybe stand closer to—"

"I'm Matthew!"

"Sorry, sorry. *Matthew*. Could you lift your head just a bit? I'm having trouble seeing your face and—"

"*Da Vinci!!!!*"

"Sorry, sorry . . . but you guys are going to want to see everybody's face."

"Just paint it already, for crissake!"

"Hey!"

"Oh. Sorry, Jesus."

It just can't be helped. The second a tender moment occurs, a bell goes off in my head, alerting me that not only is this a wonderful moment, it would also make a great photo.

I don't know if this is a uniquely male characteristic, or something that I just inherited from my particular father, but I see that I now regularly do exactly what he used to do, which he did much to the irritation of myself, my siblings, and every relative within camera range.

My father did have a genuine fascination with emerging technology that I did not inherit. I remember the first indoor flashbulbs he used with his old 8mm movie cameras. (It could have been 16mm. Or 144—this was quite some time ago.) My recollection is that the flash consisted of about a dozen bulbs—each the size of a small melon—mounted on a cumbersome wooden stick, and taken together, they gave off enough light to land an incoming Spitfire in the depth of night. I have an image of my father standing on a chair over the Thanksgiving dinner, holding up this substantial stanchion of lights with one hand, aiming the prehistoric 8mm camera with the other, and shouting at us to "Just be natural and eat the turkey." I don't recall it being a particularly relaxing evening.

Then there were the early Polaroid cameras that involved chemically treating each photo as it came out. We had to take this little pink scraper about the size of a small cigar and run it over the image with a sticky, foul smelling gel, so the intrusions to the family's great moments were not only chaotic, but also came with a nauseating toxic fume.

There were virtually no occasions too sacred for my dad's inescapable camera.

Late in his life, we were at the funeral of one of my uncles (the husband of my dad's sister), and my dad very casually pulled out his newest toy—a sweet little German spy-type of camera—and clicked off some shots of the proceedings. I remember taking his defense when he got a bunch of nasty looks and snippy comments for this breach of decorum. On the way out, he even took a "lighthearted" snapshot of one of my other uncles—the unpredictable and more free-spirited of the family patriarchs—clowning around and doing a funny wave as he left the grave site and headed to his car.

As fate would have it, Uncle Funny passed away ten days later. This photo—the last one of him ever taken, waving good-bye in front of a sea of gravestones—was suddenly *the* collectible item in the circle of family and friends, and my father was suddenly the sought-after *artiste* of the family, his persistence and diligence no longer an annoyance or a point of mockery but now a virtue to be celebrated. (Though not for long. At the funeral of the waving uncle, not fully two weeks after the funeral of the *first* uncle, my father again took out his camera, only to be assaulted with an immediate and virulent chorus of "Enough already!")

But I was forever informed by that photo and the tacit lesson involved: they may give you a hard time when you take the shot, but they're going to be happy they have it later.

WHEN YOU CONSIDER how technology has made it so easy to record our special moments—disposable cameras, phones, and music devices that capture anything at the push of a button—*not* ruining the moment by taking a photo feels downright irresponsible and lazy.

So, yes, we can now capture every fleeting tender moment. But that doesn't necessarily mean there's that much more to capture. People don't get married more, or have more birthdays, or have more kids. Babies haven't gotten cuter, kittens aren't playing in hammocks with balls of yarn more frequently than they used to.

But we've made adjustments; we've expanded our notion of what constitutes a tender moment. College graduations and high school

graduations don't allow enough opportunity for recording special
moments, so we've started making a bigger deal out of elementary
and kindergarten graduations. We film Open School nights. We film
the opening of every gift and greeting card. We record not only "Baby's first solid food" but also every dinner partner's first bite of "You
won't believe how good this is!"/"You won't believe how spicy this
is!"/"You won't believe how disgusting this is!" We film sunsets. We
film people *looking* at sunsets. We film people learning how to use
their new memory-capturing device while standing *in front of* a sun-
set. We record anything that seems important or that could, upon
reflection, later seem important or, at a bare minimum, anything
that might someday make a nice screen saver.

This kind of Emotional Event inflation can only go so far. Mod-
ern fishermen have used all kinds of complicated machinery to
catch so many fish that now we're running out of certain species
entirely. So too we may have depleted our stock of tender moments
to such a degree that fewer and fewer things feel truly spontane-
ous, meaningful, and real. The expectation and practice that everything special will be recorded has led us to treat *everything* as
special, the result being that now *nothing* feels so special. Instead,
it all feels like movies we've seen before, reruns from our own
lives.

WHEN I WAS GROWING UP, my father always described our family vacations as "making memories." We didn't have to enjoy the
trips; we just had to go, and take pictures.

I am blessed to have so many nice memories. And thanks to the
technology we have now, these memories flash across my computer
screen all day.

Next to my computer on my desk is a black-and-white photograph of my mother and father on their wedding day. They look impossibly young: he, in his army uniform, looking like a cross between John Garfield and Glenn Miller; she, beautiful and sparkling, a Jewish Donna Reed. Stare at it long enough and you can just make out the sounds of their thoughts, the excitement for the future. Knowing what will and what will not be for these two young people, my parents, makes it almost unbearably beautiful and sad. The photo captures a tender moment that I wasn't alive to experience. It's photos like that which compel me to risk my boys' irritation. One day, I imagine, long after I'm gone, maybe they'll look at a photo of their mother and me and wonder what *we* were thinking and feeling. (I can give them a hint: My wife was wondering why I had asked this stranger or waiter or bus driver to take yet another photo. And I was thinking: "Why couldn't this guy count before he took it? Who doesn't count to three before taking a photo?")

THE TRUTH IS my boys probably won't be able to even *find* a photo. Our generation takes more pictures than any before it, but if I actually want to find a particular picture, I have no idea where it is. Never been cheaper and easier to take photos and videos, yet somehow none of them seem to last. They disappear into files or onto flash drives or into thin air. Photos are becoming like pensions: something we relied on and assumed would be around forever, but then turn out, to our great surprise, to have all pretty much evaporated.

And it's not just me, either. NASA spent a lot of money taking photos and filming their trips. Understandably; if you go to the moon, it'd be nice to see a picture. Well, apparently, they lost a whole bunch of film from the moon landings. This is NASA we're talking about, not me. They captured the moment—they just can't remember where they put it.

A YEAR OR TWO AGO, I actually dug into the thousand million hours of home videos we'd accumulated over the years and decided to make a "greatest hits" video for my wife for Mother's Day. I spent weeks and weeks clandestinely selecting and editing video clips and finding just-the-right songs to go with it (because there's a fine line between getting someone a little teary-eyed and putting them in the hospital). When it was all done, I'm going to be honest with you: It came out pretty darn well. She loved it as much as I knew she would.

Though above and beyond the joy of watching her watch it (which was enough of a reward for me, frankly), I also had the singular experience of having sifted through all that stuff to begin with. Literally thousands of hours of video that included—but was not limited to: virtually every hour of the first six months of each of our children's lives, every birthday party, every holiday, every visit, every vacation, every new pair of pants my boys tried on—you name it, we had it recorded, labeled, and somewhere in a shoebox. But until I decided to make that video I had never looked at any of it. Other than when I shot it and wanted to check that the battery was working, I had never seen this stuff. And as dull as 99 percent of it is—sorting through the out-of-focus, blurry, herky-jerky parts, and the long patches where you were unaware the camera was running and unintentionally recorded hours on end of your own thigh—when you get past that, there is indeed spectacular treasure to be mined.

. . .

ONE DAY we were trying to clean out a packed-to-the-rafters closet at home and we came across an old box of photos. Some from the recent past—my kids as infants, toddlers, preschoolers—and some from life before they were here. The early years of our marriage. And the years leading up to that; the dating, the single years, our college years, our own childhood birthday parties. Boy, did our kids love looking through those pictures! Making fun of our bad haircuts and horrendous fashion choices, how undeniably corny we look waving and posing everywhere, how clichéd our family get-togethers look on camera—like Norman Rockwell if his family overate and squabbled and hated being photographed.

The hour or so that we sat on the floor of that closet—a full family doing something as organic, unforced, and joyful as going through family pictures and telling the stories—was one of the sweetest times I can recall ever spending. The sorting through memorialized golden moments was becoming itself a *new* golden moment. One that should probably itself be memorialized.

As I stood to get my camera—to get a photo of my family looking at photos—my wife and children turned to me with a collective look of disappointment. In the heartbeat that it took to register the look, I sensed that it wasn't the usual irritated "Daaadd, wouldya cut it out!" It wasn't a response of annoyance. It was something deeper, and more generous. This was them appealing to me for my benefit. This was "Why would you get up and leave this when this is so wonderfully perfect?"

And they were right; sometimes it *is* better to leave the tender moment alone.

The
Car Door
Ding

I WOULDN'T SAY I'M A GREAT DRIVER. I'M CERTAINLY A very *safe* driver—just not particularly good. For example, I tend to park by *sound*. I use the sound of me hitting something to indicate it's now time to go the other way. Those cement things that you're supposed to stop in front of? I stop *on* them. "Plenty of room, plenty of room, plenty of room—BOOM—okay, no more room."

So, consequently, my car always has an impressive array of scrapes, dings, scratches, and plastic things dangling unattractively. And I never rush to fix them, because I'm pretty confident I'm just going to bang them up again anyway, so why bother?

Plus, it's just not that big a deal to me. But it really does bother *other* people, I've noticed. I see strangers very unkindly pointing and ridiculing. They don't think I hear them, but I do. "Look at that car! There's a person who clearly has no regard for himself or anyone else, either. Look at that bumper! Disgusting! If he treated his dog like that, we'd report the sicko!"

Of course, it's *not* a dog. It's a car. But, nonetheless, when the pointing and ridiculing gets too severe, and I notice my wife and children slumping down in the seats, disassociating themselves from both the car and me, I will, in the name of community—and family—harmony, bring the car in and get things cleaned up.

. . .

NOT LONG AGO, I did just that. As I pulled into the repair shop, the guy who owns the place stood outside, rubbing his hands together with glee, knowing that whatever dentistry he'd been putting off for his kids would soon be amply funded by what he was about to charge me.

When it was done, the car looked terrific. Like new. I was surprisingly happy—for a guy who doesn't really care about these things. The guy from the shop was beyond happy; he actually wept a little from joy. (Apparently his youngest daughter had an overbite.)

"God bless ya," he called after me as I pulled away. "And keep driving!"

A FEW DAYS LATER, I'm taking my son to school, and as we get into the car, I notice a brand-new ding—smack in the middle of the driver's door.

"Ah, man . . . look at that! I haven't even *been* anywhere. When could that have happened? I literally came home, parked it in the garage, and now, somehow, *this*!"

My son, sweet kid, seemed upset that I was so upset. I back-pedaled.

"Ahh, it's not a big deal," I tell him. "It's just that . . . I just paid to have all these little things buffed out and . . . Daddy's just a little upset." (I swore at the beginning of fatherhood I'd never talk about myself in the third person like that. But—it hasn't worked out.)

For his benefit, I felt the need to clarify that cars are only *things*, and *things* are not important. (But, to be honest, when things *happen* to our things, it can be very annoying.)

"I just don't understand *how* it happened," I continue minutes later, only to immediately brush it away.

"Okay, okay—never mind. It's done. No big deal."

We drive another two blocks, and apparently I can't let it go.

"You know what I mean?" I say, bringing it up now for the third time. "It's the *timing* of it. Why couldn't that have happened *before* I got everything fixed?"

Poor kid has no answer. (And, really, why should he? This was a very deep existential question I was asking—"Why do things happen as they do?" If he'd *had* the answer to that, I imagine I'd have been frightened.)

"I'll tell you this, though," I continue, now good and worked up, my face frozen in a marginally crazy man's smile. "I'm not going back and fixing it again. Unh unh. Not doing it. I'll just live with it, right?"

"Right," my son sweetly agrees.

"I mean, if God wanted us to have perfectly nice car doors, He wouldn't have made *other* drivers. Or cars that park right next to us and bang their doors into *my* door—the *day after I just got it fixed*, right? Right!"

Okay. Done. Not talking about it anymore. Look how nicely I've moved on. And my son, bless his heart, was terrifically patient throughout all my obsessing. And kind enough to never bring it up.

A FULL TWO WEEKS LATER, I'm getting into the car, this time with my wife, and she hears me muttering.

"What'd you say?" she asks, helpfully.

"Huh? Oh, nothing—just . . . this *stupid dent*. I just . . . I'd love to know how it happened."

"I know how," she says, slightly pained.

And then, with some reluctance—but not *that much* reluctance—she gives up our son. The very son who was sooooo sensitive to my being upset about the dent in the first place.

"*He* did it?!" I ask, truly disbelieving.

She nods to confirm.

"No way!" I say. "He was in the car with me when I was all upset about it. Surely he would have said something then, don't you think?"

My wife looked at me with that certain loving sadness that only she is allowed to have. It has to do with what she perceives as my limited and, apparently, naïve understanding of human nature.

"Are you sure?" I ask rhetorically.

"Yes, I'm sure. I was there. He opened *my* car door and it hit *your* door. He felt really bad about it."

"Well, why wouldn't he just say something?" I ask.

"Because. He was afraid you'd be upset."

HERE'S WHAT I KNOW about our precious little guy: he's the sweetest, loveliest boy, who also has, over the years, become one of the finest liars in the world. Well, maybe *liar* is a bit harsh. How about *fibber*? He's become a consummate *fibber*. An impressively skilled *bender of the truth*. A *creative manipulator* of the facts. Skilled in the art of *reenvisioning*. Yeah, that's better. Much nicer than calling him a *liar*. (But you and I both know what I'm saying here.)

The boy is a brilliant practitioner of the deceptive arts. He reveals nothing. Gone are the days of "It was already broken when I got here." No more the humorously inept, badly played denials of an amateur; that would be his older brother.

My older boy is so endearingly bad at lying it's impossible to get upset about it. "Did you finish your homework?"

"Yes."

"When?"

"Um . . . Okay, no, I didn't."

He has never made it past the first volley of interrogation.

But his younger brother has the gift. If deception was a recognized sport, he could already turn pro. He is Hall of Fame material.

Playing back in my mind our conversation that day when I discovered the ding in my car door, I couldn't believe he'd had the fortitude to sit there and keep a straight face.

"He was scared," his mother explains to me.

"Of what?

"Okay, well, maybe not 'scared' so much as embarrassed."

That I understood. I live most of my life trying to avoid ever being embarrassed. In a heartbeat, I go from being mad to thinking, "poor little guy." I reconsidered.

"Okay. I'm going to go talk to him and tell him it's okay, and that next time, all he has to—"

"Oh, no," my wife says, dead serious. "No, no—you can't."

"I can't what?"

"You can't talk to him."

"Ever?"

"About this. You can't tell him you know. I promised I wouldn't tell you."

Suddenly I'm living a *Law & Order* episode. I've got information I can't use, from an informant whose identity I can't reveal.

"Okay. How long should I give him, do you think?"

"Let him come to it on his own," his wise mother says. "In *his* own time."

Fair enough. In fact, now I'm liking this. The mystery of how it happened has been solved—and that's what was bothering me as much as anything. And furthermore, my son is working through some important character-building work under the tutelage of his loving (albeit complicit) mother and his ever-patient father. Love it.

A DAY GOES BY. A week. Clock dials whip around in fast motion, calendar pages fly by, the Germans are on the march . . . Ty Cobb hits a single, women get the vote . . . Time has passed, I'm saying.

"Honey," I say to my wife, "I don't think he's so much coming to me."

"He will—in his own time," she reminds me.

"Yes," I argue, "but *his time* may be in his mid-sixties. I may not be alive for his time. I'm just going to bring it up."

She's adamant.

"You *can not* do that! You will violate my trust with him. I promised I wouldn't tell you."

"But you *did* tell me."

"Yes, but he doesn't know that."

I begin to lose my moral compass.

"But surely he knows you and I tell each other everything, right?"

"Of course, but—"

"I mean, except for the entire week when you actually *didn't* tell me, but—"

"The point *is* . . ." she says, growing increasingly unhappy with me. "Fine. Do what you want to do."

"I will."

"Just know that if you tell him you know, he will never trust me again, and I will never share anything with you again."

You still with me, folks? My *son* lied to *me*, my wife *prolonged* that lie, and now I have to maintain that lie (feigning ignorance, and if asked, lying *further* by swearing that Mom told me nothing) because if I *don't* maintain that lie, my wife will have no choice but to continually lie to me in the future—presuming, of course, that our son is honest enough with his mother to perpetuate their Union of Deceit, the core doctrine of which is to lie to *me*.

AND THIS IS HOW a "lie" is magically transformed, through love and the bonds of family, into a "teachable moment." Together, my wife and I can teach our children the virtue of honesty by being really precise about our lies.

I decide to honor my son's process (and my wife's vicious threat) and *not* bring up the dented car door. But now, knowing what I know, I have to do *something*. So I devise a brilliant plan of entrapment whereby I will "just happen to mention" related subjects over the course of the day, in the hopes that I will create such a friendly and nurturing environment that my son will feel safe enough and loved enough to unload his burden. (Or feel so guilty he'll snap like an autumn twig. I'm good either way, frankly.)

Day One of Operation Subtlety. We're all in the kitchen. I'm at the refrigerator. With my back to the family, and to "no one in particular," I casually offer, "You know, I almost got a ticket today." (That I am *lying* at this moment is immaterial. I'm trying to teach a lesson about honesty here.) "Yeah, silly me. I kinda rolled through a stop sign, but—listen to this: when I told the policeman I was sorry, and I would try really hard to make sure I never did it again, he let me go. Nice, huh? Man, I'll tell ya . . . It sure feels good to tell the truth, doesn't it?"

My wife looks at me as if to say, "You are perhaps the worst actor I've ever seen."

My older son wants more info about my moving violation. I make up more bogus details to keep the charade alive.

My younger son, the defendant, says nothing. Reveals nothing. A will of iron. I begin to actually fear him. I make a note to hide my wallet deeper in my sock drawer.

Day Two. I try again, this time electing to show him by example. I will demonstrate firsthand the proper technique of transparency and conciliatory soul-baring.

"I just want to tell you," I say, my hand lovingly on his shoulder, "I accidentally finished that cookie with the vanilla frosting. I forgot you were saving that. I'm really sorry." (Long pause, huge dramatic exhale.) "Whew! *That* feels better! Glad I got that off my chest."

I wait for it. And . . . *nothing*. No confession, no hug around the neck, no soliloquy about what an exceptional person I must be to be that forthcoming, what a great parent I am . . . *nothing*. In fact, he is now annoyed about the cookie.

"Geez Dad! I mean, if you hadn't told me I probably wouldn't have even noticed, but now I'm really upset."

Okay, so that's oh-for-two. The kid is hanging tough.

Over the next few days, I try a few more broad hints, horribly awkward associations, and elaborately fabricated tales.

"You know, son, that's like the time I broke my grandfather's favorite glass eye and felt just awful about it . . . And you know . . . he died before I could ever tell him about it. It haunts me to this day."

I almost manage to make myself cry. But from him? Nothing. The boy was unbreakable. The ultimate prisoner of war, this guy.

I decide to let it go. So what if I don't get the admission I was hoping for. So what if there's no tangible magic moment between us. Surely he's learned his lesson, and isn't that all that matters?

SEVERAL DAYS LATER, I can't find my cell phone. And that's uncommon. I always put it in the exact same spot when I get home, and I've encased it in a horrendous fluorescent green plastic cover for just this purpose. It stands out in a crowd. The kind of color that would help you find your phone if lost at sea. But the phone is nowhere to be found.

Knowing how fond my son is of playing with my phone, I ask him if he's seen it.

"Nope," he says, as calmly as you please. (If it pleases you to be a stone-cold criminal.)

I take no chances.

"Are you sure? It's okay if you did, I just need to have it back now."

"No, Dad, I didn't even see it. Do you remember where you last saw it?"

I look at him funny. But not *funny* like "I'm being funny." Funny like "I don't think this is funny." More like "Isn't it funny how I don't think you're telling me the truth?"

"Seriously," I continue, "you didn't play with it? Or move it? Maybe by accident?"

"Nope."

"You sure?"

"Yup, I'm sure."

Okay—I have to trust him at some point. I mean, he *is* my son, after all. A mere child.

I ask my wife, who, I happen to remember, did use my phone to take a picture a half hour earlier. (Even though she has the same phone, which was no more than twenty feet away. Why couldn't she just use *her* phone? But I digress. And reveal my pettiness. But only because I want you to get the whole picture.)

"I *did* use it," she allows, a little irked by my Columbo-like fact-gathering. "And then I put it back."

"You sure?"

"Yes, I'm sure," my beloved hisses. "Geez—I didn't know your phone was so precious, to be touched by only your hands. I'll make sure I never use it again, okay?"

I can tell when someone is being facetious. I'm very clever. I calmly try to explain that no, it's not that it's *precious*, it's just that "I need it, and I can't find it, I happened to have seen that you used it last, and—"

"I *said* I put it back. But, if you'd like, I will be happy to help you look for it."

"No," I counter, "I don't need you to help me look for it . . . I just—"

Now my son (the criminal) is getting uncomfortable with the escalating tension between his parents. Understandably—given that he was, almost without question, once again the culprit. Courageously, he steps into the thick of it.

"You want me to help you look for it, Papa?"

Okay, now I *know* something's up because, as nice a kid as my little guy is, he's not the volunteering type. So I ask him again.

"Okay—last time I'm going to ask you. You didn't happen to use my phone, right?"

"No, I didn't. I can't believe you don't believe me!"

He says it with such hurt, such raw emotion, that now I feel badly. "Sorry, buddy . . . I'm just . . . just a little frustrated."

Of course, what I can't share with him is that the only reason I'm the teeniest bit skeptical is that I know about the whole Dented Car Door and the ensuing cover-up. But since that evidence isn't admissible in this court, I have no choice but to ignore it and give him the benefit of the doubt.

So now I have another mystery. If he didn't take it (which, the more I think about it, he probably *didn't*, because that would make him borderline sociopathic, given the recent series of events) and my wife didn't take it (which I'm sure she didn't, because she *told* me she didn't), then there remain two possibilities: I must have picked up the phone and put it somewhere, and just don't remember (which is possible but unlikely). Or *something magical* happened. It evaporated. Spirits from beyond absconded with it . . . To remind me to spend less time on the phone and more time talking to my family. Who knows?

And why can't that be the case? I ask you. Who says it has to be my son's fault? Seriously. Think of all the things that ever were that now are not. My kid couldn't have hidden *all* of them, could he? Of course not. So clearly there are other forces at play. There are things that are just unknowable. Which is fine; I'd just like to know *which* unknowable thing it was that happened.

As fate would have it, the phone rings (the land line—not my cell phone). It's my son's friend, who happened to have been over at our house a few hours earlier, playing with my son (the accused).

Taking a stab in the dark—for this is how desperate I am—I ask him, "Hey, buddy, you didn't happen to see my cell phone when you were here, did you?"

"Oh yeah, sure," he says. "We were playing with it. It's up-stairs."

Turns out my son—at this point our only "person of significant interest" in the case—in fact *absolutely* took it and played with it and stashed it in his chest of drawers for the express purpose of deceiving me, and has been aggressively (and successfully) lying about it for the last several hours.

So now my mind is swirling. More than anything, I want to know the evolution of this caper. Did he swipe it, thinking it would be funny to watch me look for it? I get that—I did that when I was a kid. *Or* did he borrow it and then forget to put it back, and then panic when I started looking for it? Or is he maybe trying to slowly drive me insane, "gaslight" me like what's-his-name did to that actress in that movie? Wait—did my son ever see that movie? With who? And why? He usually doesn't like old movies. My mind is racing out of control.

I gather my thoughts long enough to thank the little cooperative witness friend, and with unabashed glee I sprint to my son to confront him with this new information.

His response? Big smile. "I can't believe he ratted me out! The fink!"

The *fink*, he says. I have somehow raised James Cagney. A Bowery Boy. A pint-sized thug who lives by the code of the street—despite a cushy childhood in Beverly Hills that is nowhere near an actual "street." I sit him down and calmly, but in no uncertain terms, explain to him that this was not cool.

He acknowledges he "thought it would be funny."

"Okay. And was it?"

"Not really. Well . . . a little. In the beginning."

(Which, if you know history, is how most wars start. "We thought it would be kind of funny. Taking that little corner of your country and calling it *ours*. Sorry.") I press on.

"And how about when I was walking around the house for half an hour, and I asked you to be honest and you weren't?"

"Well . . ."

"And then, I thought Mommy took it and accused her, and she got upset . . ."

"No, then it wasn't so funny."

"Right. But you *still* didn't tell me. You could have told me then, right?"

His face starts to show emotion for the first time.

"I was scared," he acknowledges.

"Of what?"

"I didn't know what you were going to do."

Among the many things I felt at the moment was *oddly tickled* that he still even had the capacity to worry about what his father thinks. I thought he had moved past that.

"Okay," I say. "Well, what did you *think* I was going to do?"

He shrugs. "I don't know."

"Okay—well here's the rule now," I say, deciding it's time to be more clear, more firm. "You are not to take my phone without asking me first. And if I ever *do*, sometime in the future, give you permission to use it, you have to put it back where you found it when you're done. Is that clear?"

"Yes."

And he looks like he feels really bad.

Which makes me feel good, which in turn makes me feel terrible. I kneel down so we are eye to eye again.

"Look," I say. "I know that was hard to admit, and I'm really proud of you for telling me the truth." (Never mind that it was only after I cornered him with unbeatable evidence; he still came clean. That's got to count for something.)

"That's not always easy, " I acknowledge, "but honesty is always the best way to go in the end, isn't it?"

"Yeah." He mumbles, still looking down, wishing this was over.

"Okay?" I ask.

"Okay," he answers, looking up and mustering a little relieved smile.

We hug, and he heads out. My work in this town is done.

He's not two steps away, ready to enjoy his freedom, when my little guy turns back and, in the most casual voice possible, tosses out, "Oh, and you remember that thing with the car door?"

I pretend I don't. It's been so long I almost *did* forget, but beyond that, I had committed to the lie of not knowing.

"What car door?" I ask—another horrible acting performance.

"You don't remember?" he says. "The little dent on your door you were upset about, and you didn't know how it happened . . . ?"

"Oh yes, yes, of course. Yeah, that was weird. What about it?"

"*I* did that."

"*You* did that?" I say, conveying what I think is just the right balance of *disappointment* tempered with a sense of "I must have heard wrong."

"By accident," he says. "I'm really sorry."

Very sincere, very honest. All I wanted from the beginning. I take him in another big hug, and thank him for his honesty. And remind him that coming clean is never easy—and that I am really proud of him.

I then ask him—only half-joking—if there was anything else I should know, as long as the gates are open and the judge is in a forgiving mood.

"No," he chuckles. "That's everything."

He is happy. And relieved. And I am happy. Feeling very complete. Glad that—at least as far as my young son is concerned—all acts of thuggery and mayhem are accounted for.

THE NEXT MORNING, he mentions he *might* be responsible for the sinking of a Japanese fishing vessel off North Korea a few months back. His mother claims to know nothing about it.

Congratulations

I WAS WATCHING A BASKETBALL GAME WITH MY KIDS. Lakers against somebody.

Now, watching by myself I might pay attention, I might not. But with my kids there, I'm more alert; I like to see what they know, what they take in, and to a ridiculous degree, I'm always on the lookout for any "teachable moments" that may present themselves. Any windows for discussion that I can use to broaden my children's horizons, and in so doing, transform a perfectly nice, relaxing activity into a source of tedium and displeasure for them. (It's just who I am.)

So we're watching the game. A guy gets fouled, goes to the line to shoot two free throws, the first of which he misses. By a lot. A remarkably ugly brick of a shot. And, as has become the custom in professional basketball, his teammates immediately congratulate him. Vigorously. Each of the other four guys on the floor leans across their opponents to cascade their pal—who just missed the easiest shot there is in the sport—in a sea of knuckle bumps, butt pats, shoulder slaps, and heartfelt encouragement. This always strikes me as wrong.

"You see that?" I ask the boys.

"What?"

"*That.* Guy misses, but everyone congratulates him anyway."

"Hmm," says my little guy, barely looking up from his Game Boy. (I had a feeling he wasn't really watching the game.)

I press on undeterred.

"It's kinda funny, though—don't you think? They 'high five' him whether he hits it or misses."

"It's nice," says my older boy, always quick to identify the niceties of the world. "They're making him feel better."

"Yeah—it's good sportsmanship," his little brother chimes in, happy to take up any side of an argument that's contrary to whatever point his father is trying to make.

"You know, I guess it is," I concede.

One Mississippi, two Mississippi, three Mississippi.

"But do you notice," I persist, "that two seconds later they're all shoving and elbowing and trash-talking? So I'm not sure if it's really good sportsmanship or—"

"Shhh—we're watching," they announce in unison.

I'm amused by their unified front and alleged commitment to the game, which I happen to know neither of them cares about. One is watching only because the Laker Girls come out every so often and jump around in very tight shorts, and the other one is watching because even if it's not what he wants to watch, it's still TV, which is better than doing homework.

A few minutes later—same thing. Another guy goes to the foul line, shoots, and misses. Same thing happens; his teammates are all over him. Fist bumps, chest thumps . . . One guy who was already halfway down the court trots all the way over to offer his condolences and earnest words of support.

You can never quite hear what they're saying, but I imagine it's like the relatives on *Family Feud* when one of their elected loved ones blurts out the dumbest answer ever.

"Name something you might find in your wallet."

"Um . . . a parakeet?"

And they all start clapping and yelling. "Good answer! Way to go! I was going to say 'parakeet' myself. Woooo!"

I maintain that despite the seemingly sincere enthusiasm, somewhere deep inside they've got to be thinking, "A *parakeet*? Are you *kidding* me?! How could there be a parakeet in your wallet!?"

But so great is our need to whoop and holler—or deny that someone just stunk up the joint—that we applaud everything, however undeserving.

As I sit there with my boys, I try to figure out exactly why this national propensity to over-celebrate bothers me and—as far as I can tell—no one else.

I'm certainly all for celebrating and positive reinforcement. Ask my boys; they'll probably tell you I do it *too much*. ("Great handwriting there, buddy. I really like that capital *S*.")

As far as *sports* go, I would say I'm not only *pro-cheering*, I'm *anti-booing*. In kids' sports, obviously, but even at the professional level. I've told my boys I don't ever want to see them boo anyone for missing a shot, striking out, slipping on the ice and getting his head stuck in the net—any public failure. My guess is the guy already feels bad enough, and public derision probably isn't going to help him do better next time anyway.

Only under certain circumstances would I condone booing. In response to an egregious display of *un*sportsmanlike conduct, I could see it. Throwing a bat at an opposing player. Kicking over a pommel horse because you muffed the dismount. Or, upon losing a match at Wimbledon, shoving a racket up the ass of a linesman. These are uncalled for, and deserve some solid booing.

Otherwise, I say celebrate; I'm just saying celebrate within reason. And with appropriate *cause*. Celebrate greatness, not mediocrity. Don't stop the action to commemorate routine achievement. If an insurance salesman has a great month, you might give him a plaque or take him to lunch, maybe even give him a bonus. But you wouldn't chest thump the guy every time he hangs up the phone, would you? No, because he's just doing his job. The man is working. Let's let these people do their jobs.

Equally counterproductive, to my way of thinking, is the now-accepted practice of interviewing players mid-game, mid-huddle, mid-the-very-thing-they're-there-to-do.

"Kobe, what are you thinking—down by four with three seconds on the clock? What's going through your mind right now?"

"What's going through my mind? Mainly, 'Man, I wish this guy wouldn't talk to me right now because I have to focus so I can *make* the shot and then we can maybe talk about it *after* the game.' How would that be, Sparky? Would you mind not talking to me right now? I'm *working*!"

AS I SAY, I seem to be the only one bothered by these accepted practices. And to be honest, I don't like feeling this way. I start to sound like the cranky Old Guy who sits in the corners at parties and lectures about how much better the world was in *his* day. ("You know, back then we didn't *have* parties. And we were better off for it too!")

And maybe my kids are right; maybe there's nothing wrong with celebrating *everything*.

I resolve to change my ways. I decide to be more like everyone else, and less like myself.

. . .

FEW DAYS LATER, I'm out having a catch with my boys. One of them throws the ball a bit high. And by a "bit" I mean "barely missed that hawk overhead."

A conventional dad might do a little coaching here. Maybe suggest he release the ball a little later. And also, maybe *face me* when he does it. Not me. Instead I use what I've learned from the NBA players, the positive reinforcement my boys so ferociously defended.

"Nice throw, son! I'm proud of you. Whooo-hoo! Atta boy! Yeahhhhhhhh!"

I go to give him a pat on the back and a knuckle bump. He stares at me.

"Forget it," he says, and heads off, steamed.

Apparently, he thought I was being sarcastic.

What Little
I Know

A COUPLE OF THINGS WORTH KNOWING ABOUT MY older son:

He will try almost any new food.

He smiles so radiantly that sometimes you actually have to back up.

When I'm on the phone, he will hover nearby and parrot what I'm saying so exactly and simultaneously, managing to be both titanically obnoxious and brilliantly funny at the same time.

And until he was about eleven, he didn't quite realize why—or *that*—he used a wheelchair.

His moment of clarity came, as these things often do, in a very roundabout way. We were watching a movie about a soccer player who was afraid he wouldn't make the team if the coaches found out he had asthma, so he didn't tell anyone. Then the mean rival guy tried to sabotage him by destroying the guy's inhaler before the big game. Of course the hero played anyway, but he struggled running up and down the field, what with not being able to breathe and all.

This was just one scene in an action-packed, two-hour movie, but this was what stayed with my son: the guy breaking the other guy's inhaler.

When the movie was over, he sat there, stunned.

"Oh my God," he finally said. "My friend in school uses an inhaler!"

"Yeah," I told him. "It's a pretty common thing—asthma, inhalers and stuff."

"No, but you don't understand, Dad. I could accidentally run over his inhaler with my wheelchair and he wouldn't be able to breathe and he could die!"

"Well, that's not going to happen," I tried to assure him. "First of all, I'm sure he wouldn't leave it laying around on the floor, and even if he did, I'm sure you wouldn't roll over it. And even if you accidentally *did* roll over it, he could get another inhaler really quickly. So, I wouldn't worry about it; your friend's going to be fine."

But he couldn't shake the image of his friend being vulnerable like that.

"I can't believe he has asthma."

And pondering *that* led him to this:

"Wow . . . Dad, do *I* have any disabilities?"

I looked at him, not knowing where or how to begin. He certainly knew his own history: that he was born three months earlier than he was supposed to. That when other kids started walking, he didn't. That he needs to use a wheelchair, and that most people don't. But until he saw that movie, he had never realized what they mean when they say someone has a "disability." It was like in the cartoons when Wile E. Coyote runs off a cliff but doesn't notice there's no ground beneath his feet till he looks down, and that's when he begins to fall.

Until this moment, my son had never really looked down. That moment was, for him, the beginning of clarity and acceptance. That it came to him by thinking not of himself but of his friend, and his fear that he could someday—however unintentionally—do something to endanger his friend's safety, *that* is the essence of my son's character; he sees the world in terms of *others* first, himself second.

HE HAS NEVER asked why he was dealt this particular hand; why he is someone who has to use a wheelchair. He does on occasion share simply that he hates it, and he wishes it wasn't so. In those moments I have nothing remotely helpful to say. I remind him that I'm with him on that; I hate it too. And that more than anything in the universe, I too wish it weren't the case.

But we don't talk about it much beyond that. We just sit together in the midst of the loudest quiet there is. In the center of that quiet, there's a dull thumping; a perceptibly pulsing emptiness that announces we've traveled to the farthest reach of our combined reasoning. At that point, we just stay there, together, until we're ready to move on.

I MARVEL DAILY at this boy's sparkling spirit and unshakable sense of self.

He was once in the schoolyard, playing with a buddy, when another kid—a jerk of a child who had been unforgivingly cruel to my son in the past, teasing him about some of his challenges— wanted to play with them. My son's buddy (the nice one) stood in my son's defense and told the kid no, he couldn't join them. The kid persisted. My son, the diplomat, then brokered the truce, telling the bully simply but firmly, "Okay, you can play with us, but you're not allowed to make fun of me." The kid considered it, and accepted. He joined them, and never made fun of my son again.

Where a son of mine would get that clarity and moxie I couldn't tell you; I know I never had it myself.

I'VE OFTEN WONDERED how exactly it is that my son, or his brother—or *any* child—ends up going to the parents that they do. I don't think it's coincidence. I enjoy entertaining the likelihood that there's some design behind it; that each family comes together as they do for a particular set of reasons. That everyone is there to get *something*. And even if they're not meant to get something out of it, they usually get something anyway. That's what a family does: it forms you. Uniquely and distinctly, hopefully in good ways as well as otherwise.

Ironically, because of my older son, our world has become more *accessible.* The universe has expanded for our family in ways it otherwise would not have. We are more appreciative and more keenly aware of every accomplishment, of what every seemingly minor achievement entails—getting from *here* to *there,* for example—and how miraculous it all is.

We are more aware of everyone around us. And they of us. Strangers are more gracious, more solicitous, more generous of heart. Partially because that's just human nature; you see someone could use an extra hand, you extend that hand. You hold a door open longer, you offer help up a steep curb, you find that extra measure of patience. It's what people do.

But more than that, it's the sheer force of my son's personality that opens those doors. He engages the world with such intensity and sincerity that he is an undeniable force for good. And I know this didn't come from me or even his mother; his particular inclinations and skill set are his alone.

For one thing, this is a kid who loves meeting new people. (Something I, myself, can generally live without.) Upon meeting someone, he will learn more about them in five minutes than I would in several afternoons, and will then proceed to remember everything forever. We've been to hotels, restaurants, doctors' offices, for example—sometimes seven years after our last visit—and my son will recall, with unfailing accuracy, the first name of the waiter, the doorman, the nurse, or the receptionist, and where they're from. By contrast, I tend to start forgetting people's names *while* they're telling me. Not this kid. He takes in—and connects to—everyone.

WHEN HE WAS MUCH YOUNGER, and wondered why it was he was born earlier than he was meant to, we sometimes joked that it must have been because he had so much he wanted to do in life, he couldn't wait to get started. It seemed as good an explanation as any.

With time, though, I've come to see there was more truth to that than I knew. My son, at fifteen, has plans to travel to (and learn the language of) every country he's ever heard of—in an absurdly circuitous sequence: start with Japan, then scoot over to Jamaica, pass through Portugal, China, Switzerland, and Kenya, before finishing up in Korea. He wants to meet the president, he wants to meet the pope. He wants to meet the guys who fly planes, he wants to meet the guys who *clean* the planes. He wants to meet the person who makes coffee (not who puts up the pot of coffee—the person who actually puts coffee beans in the ground and *makes coffee*). He wants to kiss a girl from every country. He wants to meet the lady who arranges the travel for professional sports teams. (He may want to kiss her too, he hasn't mentioned it.)

We—his family, actual and extended—will endeavor to help him accomplish every one of his goals. As we will his brother. He may need a bit more help than his brother, and that's fine; that's precisely what we're here for.

EVERYONE WHO HAS CHILDREN knows there is nothing they wouldn't do for their kids. It's not even necessarily a conscious decision; it's a capacity that gets born in *you* at *their* birth. From that moment on, you discover that you will do things you've never done before, things you may not want to do, things you're afraid of, things that may make you question your sanity. Sometimes all of those in one swoop.

When our first son was born and it became apparent he needed extra help to get him on his way, we investigated countless medical and therapeutic avenues. Some seemed promising, some didn't, but almost all seemed worthy of at least considering.

Among these was a Chinese healer in L.A. who had helped the son of a friend of ours in several very dramatic, borderline-miraculous ways—all of which were attested to by this very reliable friend of ours, and additionally confirmed by other mutual friends.

I'm willing to believe in almost everything, until I'm given reason *not* to believe. Even if it's ultimately revealed to be false, flawed, or even fraudulent, I usually find something beneficial in momentarily entertaining the possibility that it's true.

So we called the guy and set up an appointment.

Far from being the wizened old mystical-looking man-of-the-mountain I was expecting, this guy was in his early fifties, a bit stocky, wore a golf shirt from some exclusive country club, and drove a shiny new Mercedes. Okay. No reason this guy can't have a nice car and play golf; that doesn't mean he's *not* a magical healer. The fact that he chain-smokes unfiltered Camels like a pool hall hustler doesn't mean he *won't* pull some brilliant trick out of his golf-shirt sleeve and miraculously heal our infant son. Certainly worth a shot.

Though he seemed to understand us pretty well, he spoke very little English, so he brought along his wife—an attractive, well-coiffed Chinese-American woman his own age—to interpret. I couldn't be certain, but it seemed like she took great liberties with the translations. For example, the good doctor would say something in Chinese that sounded to be five or six sentences deep. Thirty, forty seconds' worth of nonstop questions/comments/opinions, which she would then translate as: "Very handsome, your boy."

"Really?" I'd think. "That's all he said? It sure seemed like he was talking a lot more than that."

But none of this made me doubt the guy's ability to heal; I was just increasingly amused by it all. Yeah, it's pretty odd stuff, but, again: what wouldn't you do for your kid?

He asked some general background questions: "Does your baby sleep on his stomach or his back? Does he seem to resist certain foods? . . ."

Other questions were more of the spooky, mojo variety. "On the night he was born, did you go to the hospital from this house, or were you somewhere else?" "How long have you lived in the house?" "Who lived here before you?" "Did anyone ever die here?" "How much did you pay for the house?" (This last one, I suspect, was not a literal translation so much as his wife's curiosity, but still—not a problem. Happy to have a chance to have this guy work his magic on my son.)

After some long, pensive meditations (which involved him step-
ping out to smoke more Camels in privacy), the doctor explained
that he believed there were some nasty *spirits* lingering in our
house that may have in part contributed to our son's health issues.
At the very least, they weren't helping. (As I understood it, these
weren't "spirits" in the traditional, creepy Halloween-y vein. These
were . . . I don't know. Older. And more Chinese.) And this guy
could get rid of them for us.

It should be pointed out that he never talked about money—and
in fact never charged us a thing. So it wasn't like he was trying to
pad the bill or anything. He was there to try and help. Of that I was
certain.

HE EXPLAINED that there were actually *three* ways to get rid of
these "spirits": the first involved putting forth prayers and affirma-
tions and asking them nicely to leave. The second option was a bit
more forceful—it involved somehow *making* them leave. The third
and surefire option—which he told us he would just go ahead and
do for us since we seemed like nice people—was to cut through all
the pleasantries and just kill the suckers.

"Okay," we said. "Sure. Let's go with that. Um . . . how do you
kill them, exactly?"

He made us a list: we'd need to get some black sesame seeds, a
specifically sized white porcelain bowl, a bottle of 110 (or stronger)-
proof alcohol, and a large, new, six-inch kitchen knife. (I swear to
you I'm not making this up. *He* may have been making it up, but
I'm telling you exactly what happened.)

When the actual "hit" went down, we were advised to be somewhere else. No problem. We loaded our infant son into the car and

drove around for about an hour and fifteen minutes, which is, apparently, how long these things take.

I don't remember exactly what we did for that time, but I do recall praying, among other things, that these lovely ambassadors of alternative medicine weren't, at the moment, rifling through our drawers and stealing us blind.

They weren't. We returned home to find the doctor in the backyard, enjoying a little post-exorcism cigarette while his wife was inside, cleaning up some of the demonic debris. The knife was on the floor, next to the shattered ceramic bowl (it was $1.98—no big deal). We were not told exactly what had happened, and we didn't ask. But the operation, they reported, was a success; the demons were gone. Our house was officially de-funkified.

Not finished. Now we had to collect the "dust" and dispose of it properly. Okay. My wife and I went around the house with a little Baggie to gather the ghost detritus. We managed to come up with about three molecules of actual dust, but used nearly twenty-five pounds of wrinkled-up paper towels, which we stuffed—with the dust and the little Baggie—into a tremendous, industrial-sized trash bag.

As I'm sure you know from your own numerous domestic demon-ridding experiences, this stuff cannot be disposed of just *anywhere*. There's a very specific procedure involved. Dr. and Mrs. Kooky told us we had to dump the evil ghost poop far from our house—"someplace out of the ordinary path" of our "travels."

Okay. So we drove about twenty minutes and found a perfectly nice little residential area we'd never been to—and to which we would now certainly never be returning.

Furthermore, according to Dr. Screwy, the drop was to be made at a "point of great energy"—a busy intersection.

Okay. So we scoured the neighborhood for just the *right* inter-section: wide lanes for lots of potential "great energy flow," but with no one there at the moment. We didn't need witnesses.

When first presented, it seemed like getting rid of this demon dirt would be akin to flicking an ash out a window. Not even; more like blowing out a candle. A little harmless smoke dissipating into thin air. But as my wife sat there with a teeming trash bag on her lap the size of a mature panda, ready to heave it out the window, this "dust removal" seemed now to be an egregiously antisocial act of ecoterrorism. But this was for the health of our child. We *must* do it!

We pull into the intersection. All systems are "go."

"Remember," my wife says just before our synchronized mo-ment of attack, "we're not allowed to look back."

"Huh?"

"Don't you remember?" she says. "He told us we may likely hear a voice beckoning us. A wind . . . Something that sounds like some-one calling our name."

(Seriously—not making this up, folks.)

"When did he say *that*?"

"When he told us to do all this other crap! He said whatever you do, don't turn around."

"Why?"

"Because! If we—ooh—the light's green! Go, go, go!"

Okay. I step on the gas, we soar into the intersection, and my wife the "accomplice" heaves the few specks of ghost crap—and the acre of paper towels encasing them—out the window, and as we shout our apologies to the nice people whose neighborhood we just violated and sullied, we race the heck out of Dodge.

.   .   .

A FEW WEEKS LATER, Dr. and Mrs. Whacky came for a follow-up visit. Our house, they reported, was still glowingly demon-free, and our son was looking rosy and blossoming nicely.

The doctor did, however, notice some "blocked energy" in our boy's midsection. "Nothing to worry about," he assured us. (Actually, his *wife* assured us, but I was pretty confident she got it from him.)

He instructed us to massage our son's right foot, "*exactly* in this spot over *here*." Not yet well versed in the ways of Eastern medicine, I was confused as to why, if his belly was the problem area, we were rubbing his foot. Why not rub his belly?

They explained to us the concept of *chi* and *meridians*. How energy flows through the body in lines, connecting internal organs to other points, so *this* point on the foot might connect to the liver, whereas a half inch over on the foot could correspond to the gall bladder. The idea that pain manifesting in one place could actually be a sign of trouble in *another* place was new to me, but graspable. And compared to throwing ghost powder out a car window, this was a piece of cake.

I did as the doctor prescribed and massaged my son's little foot consistently and diligently.

A week later, the doctor returns, examines our son, and is surprised to find the problem not yet cleared.

"You sure you're rubbing the foot right *here*?"

"Yes," I assure him, a little annoyed that he would question the integrity of my work.

"Do it one more week," he tells me. "Rub a little harder."

Sure, why not. Still happy to do anything for my child, still happy to believe that magic is at play and miracles are around the corner.

I rub my son's foot for another week. Dr. Spooky comes to the house again, and is again disappointed to find that massaging my son's foot has not unblocked the energy in his gall bladder or his kidney or his *soul* or whatever the heck it was connected to.

He steps outside to smoke a cigarette. (The doctor, not my son. My son was about twelve months old.)

He comes back in and has a new plan of action. He instructs me to continue the massaging, but with one tiny adjustment: instead of rubbing that specific spot on my son's foot, rub that same spot on my *own* foot.

I ask his wife to repeat that, presuming I've misunderstood. The doctor smiles, anticipating my skepticism. I mean . . . I'm open to anything, and admittedly, it costs me nothing to rub my foot. But . . . *what*?! Rub *my* foot to heal *his* stomach?! Now you're talking crazy-talk.

The doctor chuckles along with me politely, acknowledging that by almost any standard, this is a big leap. But he holds his gaze on me an extra moment, letting me know that, crazy as it may seem, this is indeed what he is suggesting.

My brain reels, and my knees buckle. I sit down and try to get my mind around even the bare bones of the thinking here.

"Are you telling me . . ." I can barely form the sentence. "Are you saying there's . . . like, a *connection*, between my son and me, that I can soothe his pain by doing something to *myself*?"

This was crazy, but potentially kind of *good* crazy, because if, in fact, that were true, sign me up. I'll do that all day long. Take some treatment myself which will heal my child? Yes, please.

The more I let that idea ricochet around my mind, the more excited I became. Not just for the practical applications—the idea that I might be able to help my son—but even just conceptually;

that he and I could be so magically and tangibly connected was a thrill to contemplate.

Just to be sure I was getting it, I repeated it back to the doctor.

"So . . . you're saying . . . I can feel his pain in *my* body?"

The doctor gave me a funny look, a tentative nod that suggested I hadn't quite gotten it.

"What? Why are you looking at me like that?"

The doctor then took his hands and slowly crossed them over each other. "The other way around."

Fortunately, I was already seated, because this literally knocked me back. I felt the wind get pushed out of me as I collapsed back in my chair.

"*What?!* What are you saying now?" I so wanted to be done with this. My brain and my heart were exhausted.

Dr. Nutjob gently explained the possibility—it wasn't a certainty, he was just raising the *possibility*—that maybe *I* was the one in need of some healing and it was my son who was registering *my* pain in *his* body.

As opposed to every other whacky possibility raised so far, this one I had to reject. Because this one did *not* make me feel better; this one pained me. The notion that this infant—already bearing more than his share of challenges and hardships—would also be taking on *my* problems? That couldn't be right. The universe wouldn't do that. And curses upon anyone who would even suggest that.

WE STOPPED SEEING Dr. Hocus and Mrs. Pocus after that. To this day, I have no idea how much—if any—of what they brought to us was helpful or true.

I do know that my curiosity did get the better of me, and after they left that night, I started massaging my foot as the doctor had suggested. And I know that within two days, whatever was bothering my son's stomach went away. The "blockage" seemed to have unblocked. He smiled more and slept better.

Coincidence? Maybe. Cause and effect? Could be. I have no way of knowing. I'm just telling you what happened.

And something in me felt different too, after that. I felt *lighter*. I don't know what it was, or if there was even a grain of medical explanation for it. I just know that I was cured of *something*. Maybe it was the evaporation of skepticism. Or the blossoming of some new strand of hope.

WHATEVER IT WAS, I've never let go of the idea that my son and I are connected in ways that defy conventional logic. And that after all is said and done, it's quite possible it is, in fact, *he* who has been helping *us* all along, and not the other way around.

I don't necessarily believe everything anyone tells me anymore.

But when it comes to this boy, I do believe in everything.

It's Not
Just You

T HE PRESIDENT OF THE UNITED STATES' OLDEST DAUGH-
ter went away to camp last summer. I know this because he
shared it with me. Well, not with *me* personally. He told the whole
world, but I was listening. He also mentioned that one of his daugh-
ters got a 73 on a science test and the other started wearing braces.

I was genuinely happy to learn each and every one of these nug-
gets. For a couple of reasons. First of all, I found it comforting and
inspiring that the leader of the free world manages to make time for
the minutiae of his children's day-to-day lives. We don't elect robots; we elect real people with, hopefully, a sense of *all* realities fac-
ing other real people. And I have to say: a man dealing with his
kid's braces or improving his kid's science grade sounds pretty
grounded to me. Not the type of person likely to go off half-cocked
with the levers of power in hand.

Hearing the President share details about his kids made me feel
connected to him—father to father. When he confessed that he was
oddly happy about the braces because his daughter was, to his
mind, starting to look "too grown-up," I got it. I know the feeling.
"She's still my baby," he told the world, even though the girl is five-
foot-nine and well on her way to being a fine young woman. I can
sympathize; my oldest son, who I used to carry around like a foot-
ball, is no longer so portable, shaves now, and has taken what I can
only describe as a very healthy interest in girls. I could have waited

a while for this to be the case, but I get no say in the matter. And neither, I see, does the President of the United States.

On the other hand, I'm sure the President's young kids weren't thrilled to have their personal life served up on the 6:00 news. My kids get embarrassed when I shout, "Have a good day" in front of their friends. I can only imagine it would be worse blurting it out on CNN.

But what I also found so gratifying about these presidential tidbits was seeing that even Mr. and Mrs. President find it hard to *not* talk about the kids.

My wife and I try—but have yet to pull it off. We've had evenings out, deliberately orchestrated "grown-up dates," where the only agreed-upon, enforceable rule was: "We cannot talk about the kids." Five minutes is our current record. And to be fair, that was my fault. I was so pleased with our achievement, I blurted out, "Look how we've gone five minutes without talking about the kids." Apparently that still counts.

So it gives me no small pleasure to imagine the President in the same boat. I envision the rare occasion when the first couple manage to squeak out some time together, the discussion might begin like any other married couple's, with some detail from the busy workday, the President perhaps kicking things off with something like "Boy, you know who's funny? Putin! What a crack-up!" Or maybe an intimate appeal for counsel. Like "Honey, any idea where I put the stimulus package? Is it possibly in your car?" You know, everyday stuff.

But in no time at all, I guarantee you they've moved on to the kids. It's biologically impossible *not* to. Upon becoming a parent, the part of your brain that deals with speech gets irrevocably wired into the part of your brain that only cares about your kids. (I read that cavemen had the ability to reproduce before they had the ability to talk. Which (a) helps explain why foreplay wasn't invented for thousands of years, and (b) underscores how deeply this need to talk about our kids is ingrained. Till they reproduced and had kids, cavemen and cavewomen had nothing to talk about. Post-kids, I bet you they talked about nothing else.)

That's the way it is in our house. In fact, the only respite we have from talking about our kids is talking about *other* people's kids.

We talk about other people's kids a lot. We observe, we comment, we compare. And, I'm ashamed to say, we're not always kind.

"Did you see those pants on that kid? Who's dressing him—the circus?"

"Look at how that kid climbs all over the furniture. Where'd he grow up—the circus?"

"And how about that kid's table manners? Where'd he learn to eat—the circus?"

(None of this, by the way, is meant as a slight to circus people—who do a bang-up job keeping their children safe around so many wild animals and clowns—but as a confession that I sometimes make myself feel better by putting down other people's kids. Okay? Now you know.)

It's nothing to be proud of, I admit; pushing myself up by pulling down others. The Germans call it *Schadenfreude*—"the deriving of pleasure from the misfortunes of others." (How about that, by the way? There were *that* many people being *that* petty that they had to make up a special word for it.)

As near as I can tell, all parents engage in some degree of this type of "Child-freude," which is *like* Schadenfreude, just more finely tuned. I made it up, but it means: "Comfort derived specifically from pointing out, discussing, and maliciously ridiculing the flawed child-rearing practices and clothing choices of other parents." We all do it, I'm sure of it. (If not, if we're truly the only couple that does it, then boy is my face red. But I doubt we are.)

We all need to hear about other people's struggles with *their* kids. It's why I was so delighted about the President's daughter getting a 73; it made me feel better about my kid's 74. We just want to know we're not the only ones fighting the fight. That we're not alone. Of all the roles the first family serves, the role of head-scratching parents with real-life, perfectly imperfect kids is perhaps among the most unappreciated.

For the longest time, based on no evidence other than our own insecurity and sense of incompetence, my wife and I were convinced that we were the flat-out, no-question-about-it, least-skilled parents in the country. Furthermore, never ones to give ourselves a break, we believed that all the other parents in our sphere were doing a conspicuously stellar job with *their* kids.

We were convinced that every other set of parents we knew were perfect. They were more thorough in going over their kids' homework, they set better boundaries than we did, didn't let their kids watch as many hours of TV as we did, raised kids who were unfailingly polite in public and had a far greater sense of community and public service than our underachieving offspring over there on the couch watching *SpongeBob*. We were certain everybody else's kids willingly and joyfully ate nothing but healthy foods, shunning all candy and candy-based products, they all sensibly and automatically put on weather-appropriate clothing, and voluntarily called their grandparents with clockwork regularity, giving fully detailed accounts of their numerous accomplishments, ending with testimonials to their wonderful and perfect parents, who were no doubt raised by these spectacular grandparents.

Turns out: not so much. At all.

The good news/bad news is: *nobody* knows what they're doing. It's a frightening discovery, considering how many people we're talking about. But I find it tremendously liberating. It's the one gargantuan truth that all parents ultimately learn, and of which they can never let go. That other parents out there are struggling too—and maybe even doing worse than us—is what allows us to get up every morning.

MY VERY GOOD BUDDY and I have a friendship built almost entirely on confessing our failures as fathers. To be fair, it's more like expressing our fears that we *might* be failures. But no matter. The airing of these mutual insecurities (and occasional tiny victories) has been the cornerstone of a life-changing and life-affirming friendship. An oasis of support in a Sahara of self-recrimination. Apparently, we both needed to hear about someone else's problems. To compare ourselves to an *other*. We just never knew it.

Our wives knew it. They're much smarter in this regard. In fact, this good buddy and I only became friends because our wives conned us into it. Which is not uncommon, I've discovered.

For the majority of men my age, our friends are guys we never actually picked. They're the husbands of our wives' friends, or fathers of our kids' friends. (I do have a few close friends from childhood, but they're scattered about the country and I rarely get to see them.) But the guys I have spent the most time with for the last several years have been the guys whose lives, like mine, revolve around their kids. So, from school drop-offs to pickups to school plays and birthday parties, Little League, rock-band practice, school fund-raisers, etc. . . . these are the guys I'm with.

Invariably, the first bond between us was the shared resentment we all felt for being at these stupid events in the first place. And out of that mutual discomfort, friendships were forged. Good friendships. Solid friendships. Dependable brothers in arms. None of which changes the fact that I never picked these guys. Nor they me. We just got handed to one another, and were clever enough to make the best of it.

So within this group of arbitrary misfits was this one particular fellow who, as I say, became my friend only because our wives ordained it so. It was actually a deliberate "setup," because they could have easily continued their friendship without involving us. But they both had the idea, and the strong conviction, that he and I would "hit it off" and somehow "be good for each other," and so proceeded to match us up.

Privately, in our respective households, my wife and his wife were deftly selling us on each other. "You'll really like him—he's really funny!" "No, he's not like you think he is. He's actually a great guy, you guys are really alike." "You guys'll be great friends!"

And, in response, safe within the warmth of these very same respective households, the other guy and I were each saying, "What do I need another friend for? I already have friends I never talk to. *More* would just be overkill."

But the loving wives persisted. They were determined to make this happen.

THE FIRST ENCOUNTER WAS EASY—the families got together for a bit of BBQ and kid-friendly football-watching. Probably could've enjoyed myself even if the guy was a deadbeat. But he wasn't. He was a perfectly nice, bright, funny guy.

A few weeks later, the wives organized a dinner, this time just the four of us—no kids. Again, I couldn't have had a better time. By the time we ordered, the group had already subdivided; my new best friend and I were huddled in animated conversation, as were the wives in their own corner. Their devious plan had worked; this guy and I each had a new friend.

Shortly thereafter, to the relief of our wives, my new best bud and I realized we didn't need to go out and eat an entire dinner just to talk. Or even need to involve our wives. We could actually get together without them, which it turns out was everybody's preference.

We had discovered early on that among the many things we had in common was an appreciation of the occasional cigar and a bit of Scotch. Very *manly* things—which took the sting out of the unspoken self-consciousness we were both feeling about doing something as *un*-manly as, apparently, *courting.*

So we initiated a weekly get-together—always on the same night of the week, always at the same time—for our Scotch, cigar, and chat. And as enjoyable as each of those elements was, it was the *routine* of doing it that became the centerpiece. We each found we looked forward to the consistency of these sit-downs.

And what flowed out of them was a steady stream of revelations. "Wow, my kid is going through the same problem with *his* teacher." "Yeah, we tried the same meds for our kid, but got off it too." "Yeah, my kids hate when I do that too." And on and on. A veritable marathon of acknowledged shortcomings, from which the net *take-away*, for both of us, was a huge sense of "Wow, I thought it was just *me*!" Followed by a giddy sense of excitement in the relief and fun of that very discovery.

Why men are so late to the party in learning to do this is for people smarter than myself to figure out. But I do know there is a consistent gender divide here. Women know how to have friends, whereas men, I think, don't. When my wife gets together with her friends, they will succinctly download the details of every facet of each other's life. If I go to a ball game with a buddy, nothing makes us both happier than the sheer joy of getting to sit there and *not talk* for fifteen consecutive minutes.

I remember my father being the same way. A remarkably amiable fellow, with plenty of friends (actually they were mainly the husbands of my mother's friends), but I don't think he ever once picked up the phone and called a friend because he wanted to *talk*.

I'm not saying this is the best way to live; I just had not till recently noticed the discrepancy. My wife *needs* her friends. She *cherishes* her friends. I *have* friends, but have pretty much always felt I'd be fine without them too. Sort of the way I feel about *juice*; nice to have, but if we're out, I'll have something else.

Until I had kids. Then I *needed* friends. And, probably for the first time, was able to really *be* a friend. It's another reason having kids is such a game-changer: it opens you in ways that just would not have happened otherwise. It connects you to all those *others*. Whether in friendship or mocking ridicule—either way, you need to acknowledge and take in *others*.

AND THIS IS THE CORNERSTONE of my plan for World Peace. Granted, I haven't worked out *all* the details, but I figure if presidents and prime ministers all over the world would just open every conversation with something about their kids, it may not bring about global harmony overnight, but it's not going to start any wars either. It can only be a step in the right direction. Talking about kids does that; it brings out the common ground between *everybody*.

Which is why I bet you, somewhere in the White House, late at night, you can probably hear someone say, "Hey, I'm sure the Ahmadinejads' kid didn't do so great on that science test, either."

Bad Words

WHEN MY LITTLE GUY WAS IN SECOND GRADE, HE came home one day very pleased with himself.

"Daddy, I know what the 'f-word' is."

Oh, boy. I knew this was coming someday, I just hadn't expected it so soon.

"Well, where'd you learn that?" I asked.

"In school."

I was so pleased with the public school system.

"In class? You learned this in class?"

"No. From my friend Max."

"Max already knows the 'f-word'?"

"Uh-huh," my little angel said, bursting with confidence and the need to impress me. "Want to know what it is?'

"Okay," I said, nervously. "What *is* the 'f-word'?

He stood to his full three-foot-seven.

"It's 'shit,'" he said, beaming with pride. It took me a minute.

"'*Shit*' is the 'f-word'?"

"Uh-huh."

"You sure?"

"Uh-huh."

Now I was faced with a parenting dilemma. Do I let him go out in the world so woefully misguided? That seemed the very opposite of what parenting should be about. On the other hand, correcting him didn't seem right either. "Oh, no, son—you've got it wrong. The 'f-word' is *far* more offensive. And with so many more permutations and variations. Come—pull up a chair, I shall explain." That seemed far worse. And counterproductive. So I let it slide.

"That's right, son," I said. "You've got it right. Now, you know that's a bad word, though, right?"

"Yeah," he said, as he ran off to enjoy his quickly evaporating childhood. I sensed this discussion wasn't over.

A few days later, he came over and acknowledged, "Daddy, I was wrong. That wasn't the 'f-word' at all. That was the '*s-word.*'"

"That's right, sweetie. What you have there is the 's-word.'"

He *was* learning, so that's good.

"I know how to spell it too," he told me.

"Do you?" I asked, making a mental note to get him new friends.

"Uh-huh," he said. And then, with professional spelling bee precision, he laid it out. "S-h-i-m-t."

"What?"

"S-h-i-m-t," he repeated with unshakable confidence.

"*Shimt?*" I said, making sure I'd heard right. "With an *m*?"

"Uh-huh."

I had not known that. *Shimt,* if I'm not mistaken, was a dish my grandmother used to make, generally on the high holidays. *Potato shimt,* with raisins and carrots and pieces of chicken tossed in. Sometimes beef—it varied. I had not heard of it in the context my son was proposing, but I nonetheless decided to accept his version as official.

"That's right," I said. "You got it. Now. Just because you know these words doesn't mean you get to *use* them."

This upset him.

"Why not?"

"Because they're not nice words. I don't want to hear you use these words."

"But why would they have words if you're not allowed to say them?"

"Well, you can say them when you're older."

"But my friends say them!"

"That's because your friends' parents don't give a *shimt*. But I don't want to hear those words from you."

He walked off, very frustrated.

AND I HAVE TO SAY, I understood the feeling. Nobody likes to be thwarted.

As fate would have it, I've been going through the exact same problem—with my computer. My spell check will not let me curse. Not only won't it allow it, it apparently thinks so highly of me that if I *try* to curse, it presumes I've made a mistake, and furthermore couldn't possibly know what these words actually mean.

I was writing a friend of mine who was having problems at work. Trying to be supportive, I wrote back, "Well, gee, it sounds like your boss is a real c*!#sucker." My computer didn't like this. It underlined the word in red and sounded the little warning *bing*.

"Did you mean 'coquettish'?" it asked me, trying to be helpful.

I typed back, "No, I meant 'c*!#sucker.'"

Bing. "Funny guy," the computer snickered. "That's actually a very bad word—I'm sure you didn't mean to say that. Did you maybe mean to write 'cauliflower'?"

"No, I meant 'c*!#sucker.'"

Bing. "'Crocodile'?"

"No," I typed back, increasingly aggravated. "'C*!#sucker.'"

Bing. " 'Cockamamie'?"

"No."

" 'Coriander.' Did you mean 'coriander'?"

"No, I meant 'c*!#sucker.' I'm saying his boss sounds like a real c*!#sucker."

" 'Conquistador'? Did you possibly mean 'conquistador'? Where does your friend live? Does he, by chance, live in fifteenth-century Spain? Because it's possible his boss is a conquistador."

"No, he's a c!*#sucker, you #@!$*&*%$@er!"

It finally accepted the word, but sadly the computer has never looked at me the same since. The relationship has been irreparably strained.

But, as my son has explained to me, *shimt* happens.

Enough

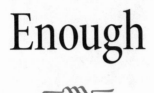

M Y KIDS LOVE ANY MOVIE IN 3-D. ACTUAL *LIFE*, WHICH is already *in* 3-D, they're not as enthralled with. But to see something on a screen that aspires to simulate actual life? They've never been happier.

To my mind, 3-D is one *D* more than necessary. I don't recall ever seeing a movie and thinking, "If only this movie had *one more dimension*! I just feel too confined by mere width and height. I'm hankering for *depth*." It's never been an issue.

But the makers of these movies prey on our insatiable appetite for *more*. More depth, more volume, more sensation, more of a movie experience.

"Detail so vivid," they boast, "it's like you're *right there*!"

You know what *I* say? "I don't want to be *there*! I want to be *here*! *You* be there. That's *your* job. You be the movie, I'll be the guy *watching* the movie. From *here*."

Remember when people used to say, "There's no *there* there?" Well, now it's worse; now there's no *here* here. It's all about taking you *there*.

I appreciate the novelty of these technological accomplishments; I just don't see the *appeal*.

"It makes you feel like you're actually *in* the movie!" my kids excitedly report. "What about that jungle scene—cool huh?! It's like the trees are gonna hit you in the eye!"

The thing is, I've spent most of my life trying to *avoid* getting hit in the eye. It's exactly the kind of thing I'm against. But now we've developed the technology to simulate exactly *that*. I would respectfully argue it's not something we need.

Very much like the new TV we just bought.

We already had a very nice TV. Did all the things you'd want a nice TV to do: looked good, sounded good, the *def* was *high*, the screen was both big *and* flat. (The manufacturers do send a bit of a mixed message with that one. I lose track of what it is we're meant to aspire to: the bigness or the smallness. Happy to buy a new TV, just want to make sure I'm coveting the right qualities.)

I had been perfectly content with our TV. But then I did a foolish thing: I went to a friend's house. And his TV looked much nicer. Bigger, better, clearer, louder, sharper, funnier . . . It just seemed, in general, that it was better to be him than me. A new TV, I believed, would rectify that.

(Deep down inside, I was, of course, embarrassed and ashamed at how remarkably shallow, impressionable, and predictable I can be. But this was, as I say, way deep down. On top of that was layer upon layer of animalistic impulses driving me, almost zombie-like, to "Go, get, more.")

SO I GO TO THE STORE to look at new TVs. I tell the guy about the one I saw at my friend's house. Guess what? They've already come out with an even *newer*, fancier model than the one *he* has! Bigger, wider, flatter, picture's more clear, tangibly crisper, painfully louder—all-around better. Ha! Yes, please. Give me that.

I get it delivered—after having completed some construction at home, expanding the wall space to accommodate its girth—and they come to set it up.

The TV is incredible! The picture is stunning! I am very proud of myself. And feeling momentarily complete.

But I soon notice a problem: It's so good, it's actually *too* good. Things look so real, they don't look real anymore. There's so much detail, it's dizzying. So much digital information coming in, so many gazillion pixels that stuff that's supposed to look vivid looks surreal and otherworldly. And oddly amateurish. This can't be right.

The guy comes back, looks at the picture, and in a refreshingly candid admission tells me, "Yeah, that's been a bit of a problem."

"So, I'm not nuts?" I ask, relieved for the validation. "I mean, it looks *terrible*, right?"

He explains to me that, in fact, new TVs are so technologically advanced they're no longer compatible with virtually everything filmed earlier than, say, last week. So pretty much everything I watch on this TV will look significantly worse than watching it on my *last* TV. The one I just gave away to my nephew because I wouldn't be needing it anymore now that I have this *new* one, this state-of-the-art beauty that apparently can take an award-winning movie of three years ago and make it look like it was filmed with a gas station security camera.

But there is hope, he tells me. If I want, they can *disable* some of my TV's fancy settings to bring it down a few notches, to make the picture look a little *worse*, which would be easier to watch. And therefore *better*. It makes so little sense that my head hurts.

Why, I'm asking you, can't we just leave well enough alone? Why must my computer offer me updates every two days? Are there really that many significant breakthroughs happening that often? Were they *so* wrong and shortsighted the last time they updated it—Wednesday? Even if the update *is* better, do I really have to get it *now*? Can't it wait till I get a new computer in a couple of years? I mean, I know we're meant to be appreciative, that we're kept so up-to-date and everything, but all I feel is *annoyed*.

I can only conclude that the computer geniuses are not doing their job properly. They seem too eager and unfocused. It's like when I see my kids finish their homework too quickly. "Done!" they say as they push away from the table, darting off to go fool around. But then they think of something.

"Oh, wait—I forgot to put my name on it." So they scribble their name and jump away from the table.

"No, wait, wait—I forgot to finish that last part." Scribble, scribble, scribble. "Done!" (Beat.) "Oh, hang on a second—I think we were supposed to draw a picture on question four—I forgot to draw the picture."

It never ends. Don't these computer people understand we're not going anywhere? Relax. Take a second, make sure you got it right, and *then* hand it in.

BUT WE HAVE GROWN accustomed to—*addicted* to—getting newer, better, faster . . . *more* all the time. And I don't see how it can ever end well.

My boys like rolled-up dried fruit. It used to come in little strips—a couple of bites' worth per serving. Now it's sold by the *foot*. I'm delighted they want to eat something relatively healthy, but putting a foot of *anything* in your mouth is just wrong.

We were at the movies and my kids talked me into getting them each a Slurpee the size of my first apartment. I know it can't be good for them, but to be honest, it's just that the cup is so big, I figure whatever's going on inside it must be pretty terrific to justify that kind of commitment.

And besides: the price of a massive amount of Slurpee is not that much more than a small. Same with the large size of popcorn or fries or anything; having already jumped off the ledge of good health and reason, why quibble over the amount? Might as well go whole-hog. (Do you notice, by the way, it's never "half-hog"? Even in describing our gluttony, we have to go overboard. You would think half a hog would be more than enough to paint the appropriate picture, but no—we need the *whole* hog.)

I KNOW THAT, AS PARENTS, it's our job to guide our children in these matters, to help them develop that muscle, that internal mechanism that tells them when they've "had enough"—of anything. But I may be the wrong person to lead on this one; from the get-go, *portion control* has never been one of my strengths.

My wife continues to be bewildered at my inability, when eating, to distinguish what might be reasonably called "a portion." I continually defend myself by arguing that I only eat "one" of anything.

My units of measurements are, however, admittedly murky. A platter of roasted potatoes, for example, meant to serve *many*, is, to my way of thinking, still just *one thing* of potatoes. Eating *two* families' worth of potatoes would be piggish, no question. But *one* family's worth? Come on! It was there, on the plate. I assumed it was meant to be consumed in its entirety, so I *did*. Why is that wrong?

Eating one muffin and then *another* muffin could, I understand, be considered eating *two* muffins. But I don't see it that way. I round up to the *largest unit of measurement*. There was a box/a plate/a bag/a container—a *thing*, whatever you want to call it—of muffins and I ate it. I ate *the thing* of muffins. I didn't have *two things* of muffins, because that would clearly be unhealthful and inconsiderate.

Do you see what I'm saying? I fear you don't. Yeah, well . . . I'm not arguing; it can be a problem. Even without entire industries conspiring against me, I sometimes have a hard time knowing when enough is, in fact, enough.

I'm the same way with *work*. I love to work. I also love doing absolutely nothing. What I do *not* enjoy is doing *just a little* of either. I tend to lean toward all or nothing.

If I'm doing nothing, I really must do absolutely nothing; I'm talking about a not-moving, staring-into-space, slack-jawed, spittle-on-the-bottom-lip Nothing.

When I'm on vacation, I have great clarity of purpose. I know what I'm there to do. I look at a beautiful mountain and say, "*That* is a beautiful mountain." My job is simply to look at it, take it in, and enjoy it. Nothing else. I don't have to climb it, fix it, or explain anything to it. I don't have to report it, sell it, talk to it, expand it, or turn it into a novel. I just have to let it be a mountain. I am very clear about my job and committed to it.

Just as when I'm working, I commit wholeheartedly to *that*. I dive in, work constantly, stay up late, and wake up early, preferably working on *several* things at once, with an equal amount of adrenaline-stoked energy brought to each of them.

As there are but twenty-four hours in a day, this amount of work necessarily detracts from my personal life.

I recently made the mistake one night of bringing a script I was working on into bed with me. I was so excited and immersed in the story, so happy with that day's progress and anxious to continue tinkering, that I just couldn't help myself.

My wife looked at me from her side of the bed with that same expression of bewilderment she has when I happily polish off a whole thing of potatoes. This look was a little worse, actually. This was as if I had brought that plate of potatoes into our bed. With a stripper. It was a *hybrid* look; equal parts amusement, disgust, and confusion, topped off with the slight tilt of the head she does which I have come to recognize as "You're kidding me, right?"

I was then made to understand by my lovely bride that either *I* could stay or the *script* could, but that she was not prepared to deal with three of us in the bed.

Point taken, I rolled up my script and headed downstairs to our guest bedroom to spend the night. My reasoning being: as much as I adore my wife—and I do—she would likely still be there tomorrow, whereas the brilliant idea I had for the script might *not*. (Again—I'm not saying this is good. I'm saying, yes, there's a problem: I can't always tell when enough is too much.)

I STARED AT THE PAGES for a while, but sadly, predictably, the inspiration had passed. I had nothing.

I tossed the script aside, and having already "made my bed," so to speak, I shut the lights and finally called it a night.

But I was still too wired to sleep. So I flipped on the TV we have there in the guest bedroom. It's from three houses ago. It's eighteen years old, square, thick, and has *no* def whatsoever.

You know what? I'll be honest with you: it looked fine.

Faith

I THINK OF MYSELF AS A PERSON OF FAITH. NOT NECES-sarily *religious*. It's not like I've even thought these things through particularly well. I just . . . kind of have faith.

For starters, I have faith in people. I like to believe that people are basically good.

But in the real world, pressure and circumstance conspire daily to cause even the best of people to behave Not So Good. So I also have faith that I will often be disappointed. I don't *like* it, I'm just not that surprised by it anymore. So my faith still pays off.

As far as the Big Picture goes, I would consider myself a Believer. Is there a God? What do I know? I know it makes me feel better to believe there is, so why not? Plus, how else to explain the splendor, the grandeur? I mean, we've had a lot of smart people so far, but I don't think any of them could have invented rain. Or an apple. Or the perfect grilled cheese sandwich. This comes from something beyond human endeavor. As Mel Brooks's Two-Thousand-Year-Old Man says, "There's something bigger than Phil!"

As to *what* that something is, I couldn't tell you. I don't have the details. I don't need to know specifically *how* it works; I'm just happy that it seems to be working. Life is short enough as it is, so I figure it's better to focus on things I have a chance of figuring out— like why men insist on flushing before we're done peeing. It makes no sense, it's counterproductive, yet we continue to do it.

As I say, I'm simple. My wife, on the other hand, is a much deeper person. She demands clarity.

A few months ago, we were enjoying a lovely walk along a lovely beach on a lovely day, when we came upon a dead goat. Not a whale, mind you, or a baby seal—something you could reasonably expect to see washed ashore. A goat. Dead. On the sand.

"Oh my God!" my wife says, grabbing my arm, pulling me with her as she inched closer to investigate. "Why is there a goat on a beach?!" She was transfixed by this anomaly.

"I don't know," I shrugged. "Maybe it washed up."

"From where?"

"A boat? Maybe it fell off a boat?"

"In *Malibu*? You see any boats going by with goats on them?"

I was defending a thesis I not only just made up, but for which I had no conviction whatsoever.

"Okay, well, maybe he got separated from a herd of goats or from his goat-herder and wandered off the road," I offered.

"From where? There are no other goats around here."

"Okay," I said, now pulling possible scenarios out of thin air. "How about this: some people, from a culture perhaps more *goat-centric* than our own, were planning to barbecue it, and then . . . got distracted and went back to the car. And by the time they realized they forgot the goat, it was too late. So they left him here."

"No," my CSI-expert wife concluded. "Because there's no fire pit, and no evidence of human activity."

"Hmm," I concede, having run out of possibilities. "Weird. C'mon—let's keep walking."

So we walk, but my wife is now very disturbed. Not by the goat, mind you. By *me*.

"How does that not bother you?" she asks, in a joltingly accu-satory tone. That I didn't share the intensity of her perturbed-ness was more irksome to her than the perturbing offense itself. "Don't you find it weird that a goat is laying there, in a place where goats should not be?"

"Yes."

"But it doesn't *bother* you?"

"No."

"But . . . Why?!"

I shrugged. "I just accept it."

I DIDN'T SAY IT to be flip, or dismissive. I meant it. There is great liberation in being a simpleton. I was genuinely okay with a dead goat on a beach being "just one of those things" that will likely never be explained to our satisfaction. So why not embrace it as a "miracle" and move on? Miracles don't always have to be big and flashy, you know.

I once had a half-eaten cookie appear on my desk from nowhere that had no conceivable explanation. I hadn't brought that cookie into the house. I lived alone at the time and no one had a key, so nobody else could have put it there. (The idea that a burglar still struggling with the concept of burgling might have broken in and brought it to me as a housewarming gift did cross my mind, but was ultimately rejected.)

And it was a very specific cookie too. Not readily available, or even store-bought. It was a homemade, dry, chalky *mandel-bread* kind of cookie that is edible only if you dip it in really strong coffee for a really long time. Like my grandmother used to do. In fact, this was the very kind of cookie my grandmother used to make. I hadn't had one since she passed away some twenty years earlier, but I was certain this was a grandmother cookie. Then, with a chilling shiver, it hit me: Maybe this was from *her*. Maybe my grandmother "visited" from . . . wherever grandmothers go when they die, and left me a cookie. With a bite taken out of it. (That's how sweet she is; she even tasted it to make sure it was good.) Yes! I was certain. There was no other explanation. (How she found my apartment, or even knew I had moved to L.A., I hadn't figured out yet. But, again—this is not for me to fathom. It just "is.")

And as ridiculous as it sounded, it made me really happy. What was at first a troubling conundrum was now a very pleasing, supernatural care package from my deceased grandmother. Is God great or what?! (I didn't eat the cookie, of course. I threw it out. But still . . . a miracle.)

AS TO WHEN I may have started to believe in God, God only knows. I don't think I was born with it. It was something I must have learned, but that doesn't make it any less real or heartfelt. I mean, I also believe two plus two equals four, but somebody had to explain it to me first.

I would imagine that, to the extent I even thought about it, as a kid I probably figured my parents were God. After all, they made me. They gave me life, and from there continued to keep me alive with food, shelter, warmth, love, hats—everything I needed.

It wasn't long, though, before I began to suspect my parents were not, in fact, God. I don't mean this as a criticism. It just didn't make sense that God would be so concerned about me and my sisters, and so much less about everyone else in the world. It didn't add up; I had imagined God to be a more thorough deity.

But I found this discovery reassuring. If my parents weren't God, then they must be human beings, doing the best they can. Same as me. So, okay—good; we were all on the same team.

By the time I was a teen and started exploring the subject a bit more rigorously, I got a glimpse of how many diverse opinions, descriptions, and variations there are of what God might be and what people think God can do, and I realized I was going to have to make some choices. A little picking and choosing seemed in order. For example: Did God really see everything I did? Not so sure. I couldn't imagine anyone tolerating being that bored.

Also the idea that there was some sort of Master Plan in effect didn't hold up to scrutiny for me either. While I was happy to understand that God created the world and all that was in it, I never really believed He was intimately involved in running, say, the airlines. Or arranging for dogs to get hit by buses. Or whispering suggestions to nut jobs to blow things up. Or keeping the Cubs from getting to the World Series. I imagined the Lord would be too busy for this. And personally *against* these very types of things. Which, again—I found comforting; if God's not responsible for all that's bad, then He's probably as frustrated and heartbroken about these things as the rest of us. Maybe even more. Which now put *Us* on the same team, too.

EVEN IF I HADN'T BELIEVED in God before, seeing the birth of my boys would have swayed me entirely. From the moment you first hold your child (and, really, every time you look at them thereafter), you can't help but be overwhelmed with the sheer marvel of it all. Are you kidding me? How can this be?! We started with nothing, and now *this*? A whole human being who can learn English in less than twenty-four months and kind of looks like my grandfather? How is that possible? And the heart and the lungs all know what to do? Who could've possibly made this happen? I mean, my wife and I are good, but we're not *that* good. Some other force is clearly at work.

It's a good thing that having children fortifies your faith, because you need it. As a parent, you get tested in ways you could never have imagined, and that extra dose of belief comes in handy. Maybe that's why they made birth so spectacular; to instill us with a faith that then gives us the strength to endure all that follows. It's like movies that have a great first ten minutes; it may not in any way reflect the next hour and a half—but the fact that you were so impressed up front will keep you there till the end, believing all the while that it will ultimately be worth it.

This extra sense of "awe" sustains us through the patches of *less* awe; those stretches of mundane tedium in which "awe" is replaced by "aw," as in, "Aw . . . I wish you hadn't broken that." "Aw . . . that is really disgusting—please stop that."

And having the extra conviction helps when your kids start asking the same questions you used to ask. "Where does God live?" "What does God look like?" "Do dogs have the same God as people?" Addressing these questions is like playing the net at Wimbledon. You don't need to *score* so much as *keep deflecting*. Keep your racket up and try to just keep the point alive. And not get hit in the eye.

Even when faith wavers, sometimes just having a good sense of tradition can do the trick.

I remember a few years back telling my boys that it was the high holidays and we would be going to temple. My big guy was into it. He loved the ceremony, the familiar faces, and the funny guy at the door in charge of welcoming everyone, and the seemingly endless supply of apple juice.

My *little* guy, on the other hand, not so much. He was maybe five at the time, and while he'd certainly been in synagogue before, he hadn't clocked that this was going to be *recurring*. He didn't get that this was a place we return to on certain occasions, and today was one of them.

"Wait a second," he said, apprehensively. "*Where* are we going?"

"You remember," I told him. "The place with the singing and the praying and the standing and the sitting and then standing again . . ." He was not pleased.

"Oh, I *hate* that place."

I couldn't have been prouder; that I had instilled in my son such a shallow appreciation of tradition and ceremony that he knew of our house of worship only as "that place"—which, by the way, he didn't like. I asked him why.

"Because!" he said, rolling his eyes. "It's so *boring!*"

"*Of course* it's boring," I told him, hoping that my clever plan to agree with him would throw him off kilter and dissipate his resistance. "*Boring* is, like, the *main* purpose. That's how you know you're doing it right," I told him, improvising like crazy. "It's not meant to be *fun*. It's meant to be . . ."

Hmm . . . I had backed myself into a potentially troublesome corner. It's meant to be *what*? Punishing? Challenging? The best I could come up with at the moment, under pressure, was:

"It's just meant to feel *good*."

"Well, it doesn't," he answered candidly.

"Okay. Well not *good* like you're used to feeling good—not like *swimming* feels good, or ice cream, or playing with your friends feels good, but good like 'Hey, it feels really *different* in here. This doesn't feel like the rest of the world feels.'"

"But I *like* how the world feels," countered my sage five-year-old.

"Okay, then," I proposed. "How about: this is the place where you come and *think* about how much you like how the world feels, and say thanks for all the things in the world you like."

He considered this for a second.

"Besides," I added, hoping to close the deal, "this is what families do."

"What—sit there and be bored together?" he asked, certain he was the first to ever see it this way.

"Absolutely!" I assured him. "It's a tradition. When I was your age, I sat next to *my* father and banged my head against his shoulder asking when we could go home. My father, I'm sure, years earlier banged *his* head against *his* father's shoulder, and *his* father did the same thing to *his* father. Nothing to be ashamed of. In fact, I believe it's one of the Commandments: *Thou shalt sit here for many hours, get really restless and itchy, and think about nothing but when you get to whip your tie off and get out of here."*

Somehow this worked. (He was *five*, keep in mind.)

IN TIME, I know my children will discover that I don't have any real answers. That I'm just another father making it up as I go along, to the best of my abilities, but always with their very best interests at heart. Sort of like the Wizard of Oz. As a father, my job is to stand behind the curtain and try to put on enough of a show to keep the kids entertained, and believing in something greater and more mysterious than ourselves.

Because even if he wasn't all he was cracked up to be, the Wizard did give the Tin Man his heart, the Scarecrow his brain, the Lion his courage, and Dorothy a way home. Did they already have those things? Sure. But without faith, none of them knew it.

So if having faith means hiding what you don't know until your kids can discover it for themselves, then yes, I'm guilty of being a bad wizard. But not, I pray, a bad man.

Sitting

W E HAVE SOME VERY GOOD FRIENDS WHO DECIDED to redecorate their home. As a couple, they divided the work according to their strengths; she did all the planning and doing and accomplishing, and *his* contribution was to not actively impede the process.

This is not all that uncommon or remarkable. I think I speak for most—if not all—of my male friends when I acknowledge that had we each never married, we'd all be living in a dimly lit apartment (possibly all in the *same* dimly lit apartment) with the same furniture we had in college. Among the abundant blessings we each enjoy for having married is that we live less like zoo animals than we otherwise would have. We have drapes, we have nice plates and spoons, and even things that serve no purpose but to just be there and make our homes look like homes.

But what I found so intriguing about my friends' redecorating adventure was the contrast between the ferocity, clarity of purpose, and efficiency with which she tackled the project and, in the other extreme, his most modest of expectations.

"All I really want is a *chair*," he confided in me one day.

"What do you mean you want a chair?" I asked. "Certainly your wife is not going to redo an entire house without *chairs*, is she?"

"Oh, no. Sure," he acknowledged. "There are chairs, but I mean . . . you know, a *regular* chair. Just . . . a place to sit down."

I found this so sad. Here's my pal—a very bright and very successful businessman—who, when all is said and done, wanted/requested/expected/hoped for nothing more than to have, in his own home, one guaranteed quiet place to sit down.

And I felt his pain because I myself have, for a long time, hungered for nothing more than the chance to just *sit down*.

I've always been a fan of sitting. Started sitting as a kid, got more heavily into it when I got to high school. You know how that happens: You start off just sitting with your friends, for kicks, and pretty soon you don't even need other people; you're sitting every chance you get—any time of day and night.

But as I get older, I find I appreciate sitting more and more. Because when you're a parent, the amount of time you get to actually sit diminishes progressively—while the *need* to sit only increases.

When you have kids, there is just always something—*hundreds* of somethings—to do. And doing these things invariably involves getting up to do them—the very opposite of *sitting down*.

When I was younger, I used to tease my father for falling asleep at the movies. I don't think in his adult life he ever once saw an entire film through from beginning to end. It made no difference how good the film was—how long, how loud, how engaging—he just wouldn't make it.

Well, like so many other things, I have, with age, come to understand my parents' side of things more clearly and now find the shoe entirely on the other foot. My kids take bets as to how soon their old man will be asleep watching *anything*. I now understand it as a biological truth: at a certain age, the body dynamic changes. After so many consecutive hours of parenting, after so much nonstop movement, along with perpetual mental calculation and intensive emotional engagement, the very act of *sitting down* is such a relief, that the body just succumbs. The instant your bones and brains recognize the support of a cushion, the head goes back, the eyes close, and there's not an action movie yet released that can stop it.

I believe sitting is very underrated. And I'm not just saying that because I'm good at it. Really, it offers everything you could ask from a physical activity. It can be reinvigorating and refreshing, yet it's restful and safe. It lets you relax and think. It doesn't hurt anybody else—unless you're sitting *on* them. (And even that, in the right context, can be good.) You can do it alone, or in groups. It's environmentally safe, it's easy to learn and can be done almost anywhere.

I even use sitting in my work. As an actor, you're supposed to have a *motivation* in every scene. You're meant to know, at every moment, what it is your character *wants*. As any of my colleagues who have ever worked with me will attest, my "character's" motivation is virtually always "I *want* to sit down."

Should my character already be seated, then of course I adapt. In such cases, my motivation is generally "Please don't make me get up."

I like to sit, is my point here.

I CAN'T SAY enough good things about it. Sitting also has a spiritual component. Do it right and you become mindful and appreciative of all aspects of the human condition. You often hear of meditative sitting poses, almost never of meditative "stand over there" poses. Why do you think that is?

There's an implied *sanctity* associated with sitting. Think of anything important you've ever had to share. What do you say? "Let's sit down and talk about it." "I have to tell you something; are you sitting down?" It's never "Get up and run around the room. Are you jumping? Good, because—I have to tell you something." No, because you know in your heart that *sitting* is the way to go.

WHICH IS NOT TO SAY I condone or am prescribing a universal life of sloth. I certainly embrace the importance of exercise and activity. However, I could point out that a lot of terrible things in life might have been avoided had people simply sat down and stopped doing whatever it was they were doing when this terrible thing happened.

As a parent, I've moved beyond *pro-sitting* and become almost *anti-moving*. "Someone's going to get hurt. Just . . . sit down" is perhaps the most frequently uttered phrase in my house.

Just as you almost never hear of a kitchen countertop running into a kid who was sitting nicely, so too do you rarely hear of an unhinged lunatic opening fire on his former coworkers while sitting nicely. It's always the work of somebody standing up, moving around, and getting all agitated. Had he remained seated, perhaps thinking and reflecting a bit more thoroughly, tragedy would have almost certainly been avoided.

Now while it's true that bad things *could* happen to you while quietly sitting, technically most sitting injuries involve getting *into* or *out of* the sitting position, not the actually sitting. Chairs have been known to be pulled out for laughs; knees have buckled, as have lower backs. But, generally speaking, once you're seated, you're pretty much out of the woods.

All of which is to say that if elected, I will work tirelessly to defend your right to sit, and vow to fight with all my powers the vast but unacknowledged *anti-sitting* lobby that works to dominate and destroy the fabric of our American life.

BY THE WAY, in case you're wondering: my friend never did get his chair either. Side tables and bric-a-brac? You betya. A nice chair to sit down in? Not so much.

The Other Woman

A BIG PART OF BEING A FATHER—IF NOT THE BIGGEST part—is giving the impression that you have things under control. That you may *not* in fact have *anything* under control is almost beside the point. Illusion and appearances are everything here.

And nothing shatters that illusion faster than driving with your family and getting lost. They can smell failure in a heartbeat. My children can instinctively tell the difference between "We're almost there" and "This is horribly wrong" with uncanny accuracy. Their mother can sense the same thing two to three miles earlier. Sometimes they bring it up right away, sometimes they allow me a short grace period to rectify the situation or to prove their hunch wrong. But either way, it's not a pleasant situation; I do not like not knowing where I am.

Which is why I love that they invented the GPS. Just the idea of a device that can calmly tell you how to get from where you are to where you want to go—who could ask for more out of any appliance?

It even gives you a selection of different voices to choose from— male, female, British, Asian accent, French accent . . . whatever you like. I use the nondescript mid-Atlantic-accent woman that's preset at the factory because, really, what's the difference? And also I don't know how to change it.

For the longest time, the directions have been accurate, and the attitude courteous and pleasant. It's been a perfect, professional relationship.

But lately I've noticed a change. Maybe it's because we've spent more time together—I seem to not know where I'm going more often than I used to—but a sense of *familiarity* has set in.

The other day we got into a little spat, my GPS lady and I. I was driving alone (fortunately, as it turns out), and as is the case when any two personalities share a long car ride, no one shoulders the blame alone for what transpires. The friction between us on this particular day was a little bit my fault, a little bit hers. (Though, I have to say, mostly hers.)

It should be noted that I don't subscribe to the cliché that "guys never ask directions." I have no problem asking for directions. I'm happy to ask directions. I'll pretty much ask them of anybody; I just don't necessarily listen to them. Or I'll listen to start with and then, just wing it. GPS Lady doesn't like that.

When you do as she suggests, things go nicely. She'll nod supportively—silently, of course, but you can tell she's pleased. Then she'll methodically ready the next piece of useful information you requested.

"In three hundred feet, turn right," for example, she'll say, with the perfect balance of civility and calm authority.

But, as often happens, I may elect to make some judgment calls of my own. (I'm entitled, I figure. It's *my* car, it's *my* day. Plus—bear in mind—she's not real.)

So yes, sometimes I take it upon myself to call an audible—based on my take of the situation "on the ground." I may see, for example, that the suggested right turn coming up in three hundred feet isn't exactly correct. I need to, in fact, go a bit past that.

So I dispense with her advice and do instead what I know is correct. (As is my right both as the operator of the vehicle and, frankly, as an American.)

Instantly, there's a huffy little silence emanating from the GPS that, truth be told, stings. I'm not going to pretend otherwise. I don't like disappointing *any* woman, even if she's digital, virtual, and easily disassembled.

But bless her heart, even with this obvious rebuff, this challenge to her expertise and ruffling of her feathers, she says nothing. She tactfully absorbs the slight, takes a moment to herself, and then, with a very dignified restraint, recalibrates and suggests yet another way for me to get where I told her I wanted to go.

"In six hundred feet make a U-turn, and then turn left."

I choose to ignore that one too, because it'll just put me where she had me going a minute ago. I'm not stupid, you know. And also, it's kind of passive-aggressive on her part, trying to get me back on her route, and it just rubs me the wrong way.

Well. When you ignore her the *second* time, the attitude gets a bit spicier. Now she's certain that the first instance of overruling her was no accident. My sudden display of geographic independence has offended her, and threatened our relationship.

The voice deepens in register, and the instructions spit out with a chilling briskness.

"Proceed to the next exit and turn left."

"No, that's okay," I tell her, as gently as I can, knowing she's a bit out of joint now. "The entrance I'm looking for is actually *this* way."

That's it. She's done.

"Proceed to the . . . Hey, you know what?" she snips at me. "Do what you wanna do."

"Now, wait a minute—don't go away mad . . ."

But there's no talking to her at this point. I just have to let her vent.

"You *asked* me to help you. I tried to help . . ."

"I didn't *ask* you," I gently correct. "I *programmed* you. And yes, yes—you did help. But—"

"May I speak?"

"Sorry," I say. "Go ahead."

"A lot of very smart people invented me and . . . No. Never mind. Forget it."

"No, no—I want to hear."

But she's too hurt to argue now.

"No, no—you know best. You don't need me. *Obviously*. We're here, so . . ."

"You're right," I agree. "And by the way," I add, trying to finish this conversation with a touch of civility, "I certainly couldn't have gotten here without all your great directions."

"I don't appreciate being patronized," she sputters, the words—even with their neutralized mid-Atlantic accent—carrying a surprising punch.

"How am I being patronizing?" I plead. "I'm just saying that—"

"Can we just drop it?"

"Fine," I say. "We'll drop it."

We pull into the parking spot, the air in the car heavy with a strained and bruising silence. Then, because I think it'll be funny—and because I'm not really so great at dropping things—I say, "So, as it turns out, *my* way worked pretty well too, did you notice? Because, I mean, here we are. I guess *my* way wasn't *that* bad, huh?"

She says nothing, but the message is unmistakable: This relationship is over. It's not working for either of us and—if we're both honest—hasn't been for some time.

As I get out of the car and walk away, I make a mental note for next time to figure out how to set the thing to the French guy.

The *Grmile*

—⁓—

M Y YOUNGER SON LIKES TO JUMP OVER, LEAP OFF, OR bang into pretty much everything out there that can possibly be jumped, leaped, or banged. With the exception of having to eat a green vegetable, he's virtually fearless.

Not too long ago, we were in the car, just the two of us, and I watched him in the rearview mirror as he looked out the window, lost in thought. He looked back and forth from the window to his arms, back out the window, a glance to his legs, and then, suddenly putting together for the first time the possible linkage between cause and effect, he said, "You know . . . I get hurt almost *every day.*"

He wasn't complaining, he wasn't boasting. It was just a moment of clarity. "Hmm . . . my shin is bruised from today, there's the cut on my knee from yesterday, this thing on my arm from Tuesday . . . Wow . . . *Every day* it's something."

And though I didn't say it, what I was thinking was "Welcome to the world, buddy." Not that I bang my knee every day. I don't. But I do believe that between waking up in the morning and going to sleep at night, there's a good chance something will happen that'll surprise me and ultimately hurt me.

This phenomenon seems to be new. While admittedly, I remember less and less of my life pre-children, I don't recall having this before them. I'm pretty sure it's only since becoming a father that I've noticed these daily "pings" of hurt. It hurts me when my kids are hurt, and it hurts me when they narrowly *miss* being hurt. It hurts me when they're saddened, disappointed, frustrated, or frightened. I'm saddened when they discover something about life that I wish weren't so. It hurts me when I see them not trusting or believing someone—yet ironically, seeing them actually being trusting and believing breaks my heart too. It *all* hurts a little. And I don't know how to not feel these things. Apparently, being a father means you get *pinged* a hundred times a day.

On the other hand—and this is a huge, enormous hand—you're also going to get *pings* of unspeakable joy. Daily. Practically hourly. From the simplest things. Like watching my boys sleep stuns me with happiness. Seeing them wake up—same thing. Watching them chew a cracker? Kills me. Getting to watch them grow day by day, molecule by molecule, I feel such profound gratitude, I . . . almost can't even breathe correctly.

BUT I'VE NOTICED that both categories—the *pings* of pain and the *pings* of happiness—both cause me to make the same involuntary (and not particularly attractive) facial expression.

It doesn't have a name, but you've seen it. If you've ever looked at your children and for a brief moment marveled at how what originally appeared on a sonogram smaller than a quarter, now speaks English and can pour itself a glass of orange juice, you've probably even made the face yourself. It's somewhere between a smile and a grimace. A "smi-mace," if you will. Or, if you prefer, a "gr-mile."

It's not a pretty face. Imagine holding a wedge of cheese so unreasonably pungent you can't un-squinch your face, but you also can't put it down. It makes the back of your eyeballs twitch a little and your head shake from side to side in sheer admiration of its potency.

My wife tells me I make this face all the time. Like an old guy who hums without knowing it. Now she just walks by me and says, "You're doing it again."

"What."

"The face."

"No I'm not."

"You're not? Look at your face."

"So?"

"It's creepy. You're just staring at them."

"But it's not 'bad' staring—it's 'good' staring."

"I know, but just—"

"Alright . . ."

And I stop. But my point is that that face, and that feeling—the powerful bittersweetness, the sense of wonderment running right alongside the equally powerful sense of just how precarious that wonderment is—I get that all the time. And I know that before I had kids, I didn't.

Now trust me, I was never an "I can't wait to have children" kind of guy. The reason we originally *had* kids was because . . . well, that's just what you do, isn't it? You "get married and have children." Because if you don't, everybody in the world nags you and pecks at you till you break down and say, "Fine, alright, we'll have children!"

AT LEAST THAT was *my* journey. My wife, on the other hand, originally wanted children, I maintain, mainly so she could buy them clothes. She couldn't wait to buy tiny sweaters and pajamas the size of hand puppets. We briefly discussed getting a circus chimp, seeing as how cute they look in those little suits, and how entertaining they'd be at parties. Plus, by having fuzzy animals instead of children, you cut out the whole "private school vs. public school" discussion. Just leave 'em in the yard and keep tossing those bananas. But ultimately, we decided against it and instead we made two little boys, and I have to say it's worked out much better.

ORIGINALLY, I THOUGHT it was nuts that anyone would even let me *be* a father. My understanding was that fathers, traditionally, had to be *older.* You know, like my father's age.

As fate would have it, when our first son was born, I was the exact same age my father was when *I* was born. That threw me. I started rethinking my image of my dad and had to entertain the notion that as much as I liked to believe otherwise, my father was probably not *born* a father. There was a good chance he started out as a kid, then spent a few years as a teenager, a single guy, newly married guy . . . all the things that I myself had been. After the initial shock, I found this very liberating. I thought, "Wow, *he* probably didn't know what he was doing either." So how hard could this be?

NOW I CAN'T BELIEVE how much I love being these boys' father. Just hearing a sentence coming my way beginning with the word "Daddy" gets me every time. Even if what follows is unpleasant, as in "Daddy, I'm begging you—please stop singing." Or "Daddy, I found this in my pants."

I think more than the *sound* of the word, it's the lingering, vague hint of a question mark before the sentence continues that I love, as in, "Daddy . . . ?" There's such hope in the air there. Because as far as they know, I've *always* been a father. So when they say, "Daddy . . . ?" the implication is, "Daddy . . . ? *You'll* know the answer to this." Which is ironic because, in fact, I don't know the answer to *anything*.

Like for example, I don't know what to do if anything happens. If *nothing* happens, I'm fine. But the possibility of *something* happening makes me very nervous.

Also, I don't know where anything is. In my own house or, for that matter, in the world. I just haven't really been paying enough attention. I sometimes say Argentina when I mean Venezuela. I don't know why, on a DVR, sometimes you can record one show while watching a different show, but other times it doesn't work out. I don't know where anyone in my family might have left whatever it is they're looking for. And—probably more important than anything else—I'm not always clear on what my wife has already said to the kids. This is key. It's imperative to know what conversations have already been had, what assurances have been made, and what ground rules have been laid. Otherwise, you're dead.

My kids not only know they can manipulate me, they *taunt* me with the fact that they know it and that, furthermore, there's nothing I can do about it.

Recently, I said yes to something I probably should have said no to, and my older son just smiled. And then, in his best "Look-how-I-can-be-cutesy-like-Shirley-Temple-even-though-I'm-a-boy-and-also-I-don't-know-who-she-is" face, he looked right at me and said, "Oh, thanks Daddy. You're the best-est daddy in the whole wide world."

"Oh, really?" I said, smiling proudly. "How come?"

"Because you let me do anything I want, all the time, even though you're not supposed to."

Oh. I think what I said was "Why, thank you!"

I DO KNOW THAT the key to effective disciplining is to identify what is most important to your children, what gives them the most pleasure, and then *take it away*. Or, more likely, *threaten* to take it away. In our house, the luxuries most frequently put in jeopardy are TV time, dessert, and the chance to continue to live with us. Usually, I start with TV.

"Okay, if I hear the word 'butt-face' one more time, you're losing TV tonight."

That gets their attention. Then minutes later I hear something to the effect of "Bla bla bla bla butt-face."

"Okay, buddy, you just lost TV tonight, and one more time, you're losing tomorrow too!"

Then you keep raising the stakes—a week, a month, and so on. There is a point, though, at which they're reasonably sure you can't back up the threat.

"Okay, you are now not allowed to look at a TV, computer screen, video phone, or any broadcast media till you're fifty-five, or until seven years following my own death, whichever comes later. And don't think I won't know, because I will."

Of course, the threat of taking away what they like only works if they really like something—otherwise you've got no cards to play.

It's like those old prisoner-of-war movies where cigarettes were the only currency of exchange. I always wondered about the one guy who doesn't smoke. This guy could never be gotten to. You can't take away his cigarettes because he doesn't have any, and he can't be bribed with a chance for *more* cigarettes, because he doesn't *want* any. The guy would be unstoppable.

With kids, though, sometimes it's tricky discerning exactly what it is they want and *don't* want. A few weeks ago we were all at the dinner table and my teenage boy was doing a great impression of a really obnoxious teenage boy who was raised by terrible parents. With great conviction I said, "Okay, you know what? You're going to leave the table right now!"

There was an awkward silence as my two sons and their mother all turned and looked at me with a palpable pity, till the younger brother finally complained.

"But he *wants* to leave the table. That can't be the punishment—'cause then he wins."

I didn't miss a beat. I turned again to his big brother.

"Oh, you *want* to leave the table? Then, you *can't*!"

"Till when?"

"Till I say so. And we're taking your plate away so you will not be having the rest of your dinner."

"I don't *want* the rest of my dinner."

"Then you have to eat it! Wait a second—which is the thing you *don't* want?"

"He wants to be done with dinner so he can go play," says the junior senator.

"Alright, then—the *exact opposite* is what it shall be. *More* food, and *no* playing."

For a brief moment, I savored the sweet taste of victory. But then a thought occurred.

"Wait a second. *Unless* . . . Unless that's exactly what you thought I would say and you're trying to trick me! I wasn't born yesterday, you know. Okay, pal, now I decree it shall be *the opposite* of what I just said was going to be the opposite; now you must leave the table and go play at once! And that is final!"

As he headed away smiling, I suspected I may have misplayed the point.

I THINK THE REASON "disciplining" will never be my strong suit is I'm always subtly rooting for my kids to win. I mean, I remember what it's like to be a kid, how good it felt to win, to get one over on your parents. Who am I to deny my own children that victory?

I remember once, as a kid, I did some dumb thing or another—I forget exactly what. I think I may have shot a convenience store clerk in Reno. Oh, no, wait, that wasn't me—that was Merle Haggard. Okay, scratch that. I think my actual crime was I lied about where my friends and I were going one night.

My father—because he wasn't born yesterday—called me on it, and I felt appropriately stupid and embarrassed. And then in a rare moment of parental candor, my father lovingly showed his cards and explained. "It's okay," he said. "*Your* job is to try to get away with stuff, and *my* job is to try and stop you. That's how the game works."

I had no idea that was how it worked. I mean, I suspected it, but I wasn't sure. And I certainly wouldn't have thought he knew it too. I guess it really is a game, I realized.

. . .

AND IT'S A REALLY *FAST* GAME, too. I mean, not to get all "Sunrise, Sunset-y" here, but no kidding—it really does go unbelievably fast. And you'd think that knowing that in advance would help, but it doesn't. Everything—the good stuff, the bad stuff, the hard stuff . . . it all ultimately just goes away. It evaporates, with no clear warning. One day you just notice, "Hey, you're not watching that stupid cartoon anymore. I guess we've moved on. Good."

But the things you *like* doing fly away too. One night a few years back, it just hit me, "Hey, you stopped asking me to read you bedtime books. Hmm . . . I guess *that's* over." Or, "Hey, you don't waddle when you run anymore—you run like a big kid now. When did that happen?"

The changes are so imperceptible. But, I suppose, how else could it be? Your kids are never going to tell you in advance, "You know how I can't get off the sofa without jumping over the coffee table and banging my knee every time? I'll be outgrowing that next month. And also, how I call my brother 'butt-face'? End of July—done."

It never works like that. Nowhere along the growth curve do kids announce, "Dad, Mom, y'see this little fleshy part of my thigh that's soft and still somewhat toddler-esque? Well take a good look, because that's all changing Wednesday at three." No one tells you that, but come Wednesday, sure enough, that's all gone.

SO, AS IT TURNS OUT, my father *did* know what he was doing. His game plan was simple but on the money. "*You* be the best kid you can be, *I'll* be the best father I can be, and let's see what happens."

And what happens is: *ping, ping, ping, ping, ping!*

But the good news is: ultimately, they're really all "good" *pings*.

And given that anything and everything could be gone by Wednesday, all we can do, I've decided, is try to pay attention Tuesday.

Life and
Death

—◠◠◠—

I'M A BIG FAN OF LIFE, NOT SO MUCH OF DEATH. AS THE proud co-creator of two terrific human beings, I am proud of having contributed tangibly and positively to the former and, as far as I know, have never done anything to cause the latter.

I try to avoid even thinking about death, as a rule, mainly because it's depressing, but also because—why? Nothing good comes of it, really, unless the thinking time is spent re-imagining your life entirely so it can then be put to much better use than whatever it is you've been doing up till now. Otherwise it's just wasted, anxiety-provoking time you never get back.

But just as death comes on its own wacky, unpredictable schedule, so too can the very *discussion* of death. It just creeps up on you, sometimes, out of the blue.

The other day I was enjoying a perfect, sunny afternoon with my older son, blessedly oblivious to any Big Questions, when he chimed in with: "Daddy, I really want to speak at your funeral."

I got to say: I wasn't expecting that. I was touched, but also worried. Did I miss a meeting? Had my doctor's office called with some unsolicited bulletins? And why would they have told my son and not me? Or worse, maybe there was some nefarious plot afoot and my days were numbered—and he was in on it.

After I caught my breath, I realized the kid probably didn't have any inside information, and was more than likely not involved with a family-wide conspiracy. He was just feeling loving. Yes, maybe he was expressing it a little dramatically, but still, it was very nice.

But I could see he had already moved on—his mind was racing, headed for deeper, more troubled waters.

"Wait a second, Dad. *You're* still going to speak at *my* funeral, right?"

Now I'm even more nervous. Why was he thinking about his own funeral? And why would he think I'd still be around for it? Had *he* been to the doctor lately? How many meetings are going on in my house that no one is inviting me to?

As all this is going through my mind, my son is just staring at me, waiting for . . . something. I tried to explain to him that unfortunately, this was one of those "either/or" situations. We can't both go to each other's funeral. And I had no intention of still being alive for *his* because he was going to live for, like, forever, whereas I might not make it through this conversation. I get to go first. That's how it works with parents and kids.

Nice. A decent handling of a thorny subject, I thought. His response—"Not always. Sometimes kids die."

Was he trying to kill me *today*? I mean, how badly did he want to speak at my funeral?

Doggedly, I tried to explain to my son that in an "ideal" world—well, not really ideal so much as "in the natural course of events"—the young outlive the old; children hang around after their folks leave. Anything else would just be wrong, not to mention too painful to bear or even consider, though every parent I know has some daily passing, fleeting image of exactly that nightmare scenario. I didn't mention this to my son. Instead I just smiled reassuringly and told him that he'd outlive me by plenty, and that's exactly as it should be, so there was nothing to worry about.

He seemed to accept this for a moment, but then I could see it in his eyes; this "natural order of things" didn't appeal to him at all. Because it would mean being alive *without me* being around. Not that I'm such a treat, but because for good or for bad, I'm his dad.

I REMEMBER the first time I heard that parents die. I was about five. I remember very vividly my mother telling me about something that happened years earlier, and in the most casual of tones, she said, "Yeah, I think that was a little after my father died."

I was shocked. I mean I knew she used to have a father, and that he wasn't around anymore. But I had never done the math and seen that for him to be *dead*, he had to have, at some point, *died*. He had to have transitioned, somehow, from "alive" to "not so alive." And my mother had, since then, become somehow okay with that. "A little after my father died" was how she said it. So matter-of-fact. Like "It's supposed to rain Tuesday." As if having her dad die was *acceptable*. As if life could continue beyond that. This boggled my five-year-old mind.

WELL, I'M OLDER NOW. I've had losses of my own. I get it. But as I gazed at my barely adolescent son, I hated the idea of him ever having to say, "This was a little after my father died." I know him; he'd hate that.

So then how do I spare him from that? Only two ways I could think of: I could live to be a thousand—though I've spoken to my doctor, and for this to happen, I'd have to seriously cut down on meat and dairy. But at least by outliving my son's old age, I could spare him the pain of having to be the one left behind.

Or Option B—going entirely the other way—to guarantee that I outlive him, I could take him down myself. Which is not only the thought of an insane person, it also, admittedly, looks very bad on the police report. "Well, truth be told, Officer, I couldn't stomach the idea of my boy having to be that sad, so I, you know . . . had him taken out."

Sure, that's less than stellar parenting. But I know my kids; they get upset when the cable goes out. I don't want to imagine them dealing with *me* going out.

THE CONCEPT OF SACRIFICE on your children's behalf is instinctive, and non-negotiable. I shake my head in bemusement when flight attendants tell you, "In the event of any sudden loss of oxygen, put your mask on first, *then* your children's." That's just never going to happen. I'm willing to bet money that whoever came up with that rule does not have kids.

The idea of putting myself before my children goes against every molecule in my body. (With one exception: if it's late at night and I'm hungry. There have been a few incidents, I confess, when there was one really good cookie left, and even though I knew my kids had their eye on it, I ate it and rationalized that they were asleep and would probably never notice. And if they did, I'd just tell them the truth: "I think Mom ate it.")

But otherwise, forget it. I could never put myself before my children. The depth of love and animalistic protectiveness that we develop as parents is staggering. It becomes the very currency of your life. The hypothetical measure of your limits as a human being.

Example: I'm working out. I'm exhausted and want to be done. But I owe seven more sit-ups. My body tells me it's impossible.

Maybe I can squeeze out one more. Conceivably two. But seven? Humanly impossible. What do I do? I imagine someone threatening my children. I envision, for example, Vikings holding my kids over a cliff, dangling them by their ankles and threatening to let go unless I finish the sit-ups. Guess what? I sit up pretty fast. Seven times in a row. It can be done; you just need the motivation.

And nothing motivates like the threat of misfortune befalling your child. It's a sick game, but I daresay we've all played the occasional round of "What Would You Do If Your Child's Life Depended On It?" Would you jump naked into the filthiest of rivers and swim to the other side? Splash! You betya. Would you eat whatever that dead thing on the side of the road is? Gimme a fork and pass the ketchup! Not even a question; you bet I'd do it. When it comes to your children, all is possible.

Now. Would you do the same for your spouse? Hmmm . . . let me think for a second. Hmmm. Well, we certainly don't love our spouses any *less*, but perhaps we love them a little *differently*. Neither of you would ever say you love your children more than you love each other. (You may think it—you're just not allowed to ever say it out loud.)

I don't question for an instant my wife's love for me. I also don't underestimate the speed with which she'd throw me under a speeding bus to protect our children. As I would her, I imagine. (Though I'm already preparing my excuses should the bus happen to stop on its own before impact. "My bad. It's just that the bus was moving so fast, and it was so yellow and everything . . . I thought you were someone else. But look—the kids are fine!")

Is there any force on earth as compelling as a parent's vigilance? Our children turn us into the true animals we forget we are. And that ferocity kicks in at the very moment of their birth. They pop into the world, and at first glimpse, you're hooked. "Hi, nice to meet you, I'll be your father, and I will have your back from this moment on."

SHORTLY AFTER your kids are born, you realize your responsibility for them includes becoming more responsible about *yourself*. To whatever extent, for example, you ever considered bungee jumping, motorcycle racing, or shark-wrestling, you now reconsider. You weigh whatever thrill you imagine those activities will bring you against the thought of your kids discussing your demise. "Yeah, I'll miss him, but he sure showed that shark a thing or two, huh?" (Ironically, the shark's take on it is "Y'know, I wouldn't have even bothered with the guy but he got a little too close to my kids.")

It's hard, though, to be perfectly responsible and absolutely disciplined all the time. I think I've mentioned I enjoy the occasional cigar, knowing full well it's not that good for me. Less healthful than, for example, tomato juice. But I'd always convinced myself that I was protected by my moderation, my pretty healthy lifestyle absent that one vice, and the belief that God will be kind to me because I've been, by and large, a nice guy.

Not the best plan, I admit. But it was working for me. And I always imagined that once I had kids, I'd stop. (I wonder if that's where they got the tradition of handing out cigars upon the birth of a child. Maybe it wasn't so much a gesture of celebration as an act of house cleaning. "Here. I'm not allowed to have these anymore—*you* take 'em.")

Surprisingly, though, having children didn't make me give up the cigars. I just ratcheted up the rationalizations and qualifiers.

"Okay, I'll never smoke *near* the kids, or in a room they're going to be in later, I'll cut way down, and when they're old enough to call me on it, I'll stop." (Figured I'd put a little of the onus on them. Use my bad habits as a teachable moment, y'see. Let them discover the joy of empathy and concern for others.) And I was certain that I'd never be able to withstand the pressure.

To my surprise, I've withstood it pretty good.

"Daddy, aren't cigars bad for you?"

"Yes, but not like cigarettes. Or napalm. Those are *really* bad. These are less bad."

"But, still . . . they're bad for you, right?"

"Well, yes, but . . . I had salad earlier. So, all in all, there's nothing to worry about."

It's amazing what reasonably intelligent adults can justify. I have a friend who shared that he doesn't always buckle his seat belt when driving. He finds it an inconvenience. "Short distances only," he feels compelled to qualify. "To the store. And only on surface streets; on the freeway I always buckle up. Always."

This is the same friend, by the way, who fanatically never eats carbs. "I see," I said to him. "So you'll risk death on the way to dinner, but when you get there, you won't eat the rolls."

TRY AS I MIGHT to ignore the reality of an ultimate death, I do periodically make vague, halfhearted attempts to account for the possibility.

Like when we travel, my wife and I always fly separately, the logic being that while some terrible fate might befall *one* of our planes, there's much less of a chance fate would stick it to *both* of us. On the same day. So this way, at least one of us will be there for the kids.

When we travel with the kids, however, we all travel together. Somehow we decided—while never quite articulating it—that if God forbid we all go down together, "being together" would take the sting out of the part about "going down." If tragedy should strike, at least we wouldn't have to bear the blow of losing one another. Others may grieve and miss us, but we'd be spared all that because . . . well, we'd be dead.

And these statistical considerations and precautions are made surprisingly devoid of emotion or lengthy deliberation. They're just things to consider when you're a parent. Like inheritance.

That's something I've yet to see anyone deal with comfortably or particularly successfully: the eternal question of "who gets what when you die."

There are many things you hope you impart to your children: a set of morals and values, for example. A healthy balance of self-confidence and openhearted humility would also be nice. You may or may not succeed in any of this, but either way, nobody's going to fight over it.

But your money and everything you have is another matter. This is the stuff of which family dramas are born. If not handled properly, this is exactly what causes loving families to deteriorate and gives surviving children all they need to resent one another and squabble well into old age.

There are several schools of thought on how to handle these things. Some parents believe in giving their children everything immediately upon their passing. Divide everything equally, and just pass it along. A reasonable approach, but not without its pitfalls. Divvying up "stuff" equitably is not so easy. Some stuff carries more emotional attachment. One kid always loved that painting over Grandma's couch, another kid may covet that watch Uncle Momo left us. One kid may want the living room rug, others may want to stay well clear of the rug because they know what happened on that rug when Mom and Dad were in Mexico that time.

My own parents started twenty years ago asking my sisters and me to start "tagging" stuff—so we "wouldn't fight" when they were gone. Ironically, nothing bonded my siblings and me as forcefully as the mutual disinterest we had in almost all of our parents' stuff. "You want the painting of the clowns in the park? Yeah, me neither."

We were united in our conviction that when the time came, some nice Home for the Elderly would be getting more paintings of flowers and more chairs that wobble than they could shake a stick at—courtesy of us, the executors of our parents' estate.

On the other extreme, I know people who have lots of money and are convinced that the best thing they can do for their children is to not give it to them. I understand the reasoning; give your children the joy of earning it themselves and, at the same time, spare them the burden of dealing with it. But I notice that surviving children, as a rule, seem to opt for the "please burden me" plan. It's a pain they're willing to endure.

No matter what, there are problems.

Some parents will leave their money to charity, and to the children go only the personal effects. The "heirlooms." A lovely gesture, for sure. But this can lead to even uglier displays of discontent. "Really? American Cancer Society gets all the dough and we get the Broadway show-tunes records and a ceramic vase? How is that fair?"

Then there's the middle-ground "slow leak" approach: Leave *everything* to the children, but dole it out at such a glacial pace that the "children" are sixty-five before they get their hands on any real money, and by that point, they're well into planning their own estate and seeing how they can tease *their* children.

The more I consider it, though, the more I think this may be the way to go: delay the decision and make it the kids' problem. In the case of my sweet but anxious son, it would at the very least give him something to talk about in that speech he's so eager to deliver at my funeral.

I'M NOT SURE exactly how I left it with him, by the way. I think I told him he needn't worry about funerals anytime soon, but if there's something he felt he wanted to say, why not say it *now*, so I could enjoy it? (Or defend myself, as the case may be.)

And as far as his invitation for me to speak at *his* funeral, same deal; whatever flowery, glowing sentiments I might want to impart, I'm going to share them now while we can both enjoy them, together. Everything that's great about him, I'm going to tell him today and tomorrow and every day as those things spring to mind. There's no gain in saving them; they're meant to be given away.

And same goes for the material goods, I've decided. Give them all away now.

Which is why every morning, I give each of my children a glowing compliment, a check for $45, and some knickknack from my parents' house that I never knew what to do with. Let *them* figure it out.

Castle Walls

I CAME HOME ONE DAY TO FIND SOME PEOPLE IN MY house I never saw before. Two women and a kid. Eating and frolicking, laughing and casually putting some stuff into bags.

It turned out the kid had been over at the house playing with my son, his mother was there now to pick him up (it was his stuff she had been packing up), and the other woman . . . I'm still not sure. Their cousin, maybe? I don't know—but she was with them. My wife came in from the other room and explained the whole thing to me.

So while I was relieved they weren't, as I'd first feared, a marauding band of remarkably cocky prowlers, and had in fact been granted legal access to my home, I've got to be honest: I still wasn't thrilled with the whole thing.

IN DAYS OF OLD, kings built castles. They'd secure themselves and their families behind the strongest, thickest, highest, most impenetrable walls they could build, then put soldiers up on top to be *extra* safe.

Even this wasn't enough. They'd also build a moat around the perimeter of the castle, and inside the big wall they'd erect still *more* walls; a series of ever smaller concentric walled circles, surrounding the central, walled residential quarters—generally consisting of the royal bedrooms, the royal TV room/den area, and a small kitchenette.

Should any undesirables from the outside world manage to elude the guards on the walls and then get past the crocodiles, eels, and dragons of the moat, the castle family would fall back and lock themselves behind the next set of walls. At this point, the hope (though rarely realized) was that upon arriving at the third or fourth set of walls, the intruders would screech to a halt, slap their foreheads, and then—embarrassed for having been so oblivious to the fact that they were unwelcome—turn and leave of their own volition and sense of propriety, leaving the king and queen and royal offspring safe and undisturbed.

Hence the expression "A man's home is his castle."

TODAY, NOT TOO MANY PEOPLE live in castles, but the theory remains the same. A condo or an apartment can be a castle too. So can a tent, or a yurt. Or even a nastily worded "Keep Away" sign taped to a big cardboard box. You just need some sort of marker; some delineation that says, "*This* side is me and mine, *that* side is you and yours." Your castle is what protects and keeps the people you love *inside*, while keeping everything bad—rain, sleet, snow, invading armies, bears—*outside*.

And here's the best part: it's *your* castle, so *you* get to decide who gets in and who doesn't. It's like the greatest clubhouse in the world.

Personally, I don't like too many people in my castle. You know how they say, "There's safety in numbers"? Well, to me, it's a very *small* number that provides that safety.

It's not always easy to know who it is we should be keeping out. So really, the safest thing you can do, I say, is expect the worst and refuse entry to everyone not closely tied to you biologically. My family has rejected this plan as "unworkable."

So we've broadened our admission policy.

Grandparents? Always welcome. (But let's say for no more than a week at a time, and never grandparents from opposing fiefdoms visiting at the same time.)

Siblings of the king and queen? Absolutely. *Children* of these siblings? Of course. *Our* castle is *your* castle. But boundaries have to be established here too. Castle access, for the most part, should not be open-ended, or scheduled too closely to visitations from *other* outsiders—welcome though they all may be.

Furthermore, it's generally wise to deny or strongly discourage castle access during the heavy-homework days. Or flu season. Or if either the king or queen is "just not up to it" and feels so moved to use his or her highly charged veto powers. (Which, while entirely enforceable, are not to be used casually, as consequences can be ugly—both inside and outside the castle walls.)

But castle visitations are, of course, never limited to just family members. There are countless *friends* of the court. And the friends' children. How about your *children's* friends? And, by extension, the *families* of your children's friends? Let 'em all in, I say! What's a castle for if not to bid welcome to friends, that they may partake in the bounty of your kingdom?

But not *all at the same time*. Their visits too have to be scheduled intelligently. I mean, you can't just let *anybody* into your castle. Because then it stops being a castle and becomes a Starbucks. (And even Starbucks will throw people out now and then—though always with a smile and often with a free cup of coffee.)

Castles have walls and doors for a reason. You've got to use them now and then.

THERE ARE ALL KINDS of social norms that make castle visits very tricky. Once they've been to your castle, people generally feel the need to reciprocate. And conversely, if other people have invited you into *their* castle, the pressure to have them over to *your* castle becomes profound.

Truth be told, I'd gladly give up visitation rights to pretty much every other castle in the world if it meant I could withdraw invitations to have them over to mine. My wife points out that this makes me seem somewhat unwelcoming, perhaps even a borderline *shut-in*. I don't see it that way. All curmudgeonly and antisocial behavior notwithstanding, there is darn good reason to maintain vigilance when it comes to who and what gets past your castle gates.

Not that I believe marauding armies or bears are circling the castle. Or that visiting friends and loved ones intend us any harm. But that doesn't mean harm can't happen.

Sometimes it's *emotional* harm; grazing slings and arrows of criticism or insult, which can, in fact, be harder to defend against than flaming javelins and hurling cauldrons of hot oil, because these verbal attacks are staged from *within* the castle walls, by people you've already let in. You're unprepared for assault.

"So, uh, Buddy . . . What, did you—put on a little weight?"

"Boy, your kids sure watch a lot of TV."

"You let him have that much sugar so close to bedtime?"

First of all, who asked you? And second of all, shut up. You have something you want to say? Say it in *your* castle. Don't be bringing your opinions into *my* castle.

I have an old friend I hadn't seen in years visit from out of town. Naturally, he was invited up to the castle. As we sat at my kitchen table enjoying a few hefty mugs of ale, a side of mutton, and some hearty bonhomie, the conversation turned to a movie I had recently worked on and of which I was very proud. I noticed my manor guest grinning.

"What's so funny?" I asked him.

"Oh . . . nothing," he said. "It's just . . . I have a friend at work. He said in his whole life, he never enjoyed a movie less than yours. *Hated* that movie."

Okay. I hadn't seen that coming.

"It's funny," he continued. "He doesn't know you and I are friends."

Well, first of all, I thought to myself, it's not *that* funny. And second of all, again: use some discretion, you jackass; don't share that with *me*.

Not that his idiot friend at work—or my idiot friend himself— isn't entitled to his opinion; just don't be bringing it inside my castle. Because when a person is inside his own castle, his armor is off; he's vulnerable to attack. The heart is exposed. So if you're a castle guest, embraced in the warmth of the castle keeper's hospitality and open-armed trust, you cannot violate that trust, or you will be attacked in return. Perhaps not a full, armed assault, but a gentle smack in the head isn't out of the question. At bare minimum, you are less likely to be welcomed back to that particular castle.

I'm telling you: once you open those gates, you never know what nasty stuff will come blowing in. It doesn't even have to come from actual visitors. Evil can wend its way in *electronically*. Ever go online and read one too many "readers' comments"? It's not good. You don't want every nutty opinion, every horror story, every repulsive yet hard-to-forget-you-saw-it image getting into your head, your home, your soul. You've got to maintain those lines of demarcation. That's why people remove their shoes before entering the home. It's not about keeping the carpets clean; it's about leaving the outside world outside, and honoring the sanctity of everything inside.

THE OLDER I GET, the more I find I treasure this sanctity—and relative safety—of my castle. Sometimes, staying home and shutting those doors sure feels like the way to go. But ultimately, we can't do that forever. We need to go out in the world. And we need to bring some of the world back to our home.

So what's a reasonable king to do? You build the best castle you can, but you still have to open those gates. You want your castle to be safe, but not suffocating. Welcoming, but not vulnerable. You want the good stuff in and the bad stuff out. A moat won't cut it. (Plus, my wife has shot down the idea repeatedly.)

What we need is something subtler; a defense more nuanced in its give-and-take. We need a *membrane*. A *semi-permeable membrane*, like living cells have. And mitochondria. (Gee, I hope my ninth grade science teacher is reading this.) What we need is *that*, but around our home; a protective outer shield that lets your castle breathe and expand naturally. A delineated perimeter that continually and judiciously admits and rejects, absorbs and expels whatever it must to survive. It lets in warmth, love, support—all things Good—while at the same time protects your family against all things Bad: outside invaders, unsolicited opinions, germs, and, again, bears.

The trick, of course, is having the membrane distinguish Good from Bad, Helpful from Destructive, Dastardly from Perfectly Nice.

Bears look like bears, invading armies look like invading armies. But good friends can look a lot like not-such-good friends. Nice cousins look, to the naked eye, very much like cousins who start-out-nice-but-stay-too-long-and-along-the-way-you-learn-some-details-about-their-personal-life-you-wish-you-hadn't. Discerning what's what is not always easy to do.

My solution? Again: get *small*. We've gotten into a custom in my house. Well, not a *custom* per se, but once in a while we . . . Okay, we've done it twice, but I really like it. We do this thing where we huddle up—my wife, my boys, and me—and we put our heads literally together, forehead to forehead to forehead to forehead. We put arms around each other and take a moment to lock in; to remember that this particular, quirky, remarkably imperfect foursome is, in fact, all we have, and all that matters. If all is well inside this huddle, all will be well going forth. Until, of course, it's not. But at such time, we can always re-huddle and once again re-fortify in the solidity of our bonds.

Generally, we stay huddled for about fifteen, twenty seconds, at which point the kids get restless and my wife feels compelled to get on with her day. And to stand up straight.

Me? I could stay in that huddle all day. I don't need a castle any bigger than that. It's the most glorious and empowering fortress I could ever imagine.

My Dog's
Father

I NEVER MET MY DOG'S PARENTS. WE GOT HIM WHEN HE was six weeks old. So, in many ways, I've been the father he never had. To this day, I don't think he even knows he's adopted. Our bond is mighty and unshakable. His whole life, I have been like a father to him. And he, in turn, has been like a dog to me.

And in every way, a perfect dog. A chocolate Labrador, named Bosco in honor of his color and my favorite syrup growing up, he is eminently loyal, attentive, and affectionate. When I come home, he bounds over and buries his face in my crotch. No one—and I mean *no one*—else has ever done that for me.

He's a loyal and fearless protector of our home and family. If a car drives within a hundred feet of our door, he is there instantaneously, barking ferociously and ceaselessly until he determines the person to be friend or foe. Though I have to say, I don't quite understand his vetting process. He barks at everyone—whether he's seen them every day for years or never met them in his life. But upon the door opening, he is instantly the new arrival's best friend—tail wagging, shamelessly whimpering and ready to play. There is not even a second of evaluation going on, near as I can tell, which makes me wonder what all the barking and "mean dog" posturing is all about. I've decided that, given his sweet nature, the barking is not the result of perceived danger but rather his sheer frustration in not being able to personally greet the guest sooner.

The big, stupid door is not letting him do his job. Because once that barrier is removed, he rockets out the door and invariably lavishes upon the visitor his boundless love. This is how sweet an animal he is.

He sleeps in our bed, generally right between my wife and me. I don't always want him to, but I lack the ability to deny him.

He will never, ever be the one to break from a hug or a scratch. He would have you rub his ears literally until one of you expires.

He loves our children and knows their individual habits and idiosyncrasies. He knows when to approach and when to give them their space. He knows which is more likely to drop a piece of cookie, which one perhaps some chicken. If ever he is not sleeping in our bed, it's because he's posted himself as sentry outside the boys' rooms—equidistant between the two, ready to snuggle or protect either in a heartbeat. On the rare occasion that the boys are away for the night, Bosco will again place himself right outside their rooms, awaiting their safe return.

No one could ask for a more wonderful dog.

HE'S EIGHT NOW. By no means a puppy, but still vibrant, active, and healthy. A happy, contented dog by any measure. Yet I sense something changing; he's not the same dog of a few years ago.

A little while back, Bosco and I were sitting in our favorite spot in the backyard, watching the squirrels. Very interesting critters, squirrels. On this particular day, two squirrels were busily darting back and forth shuttling what looked to be building supplies— twigs, branches, a buzz saw, and an orange vest. They were very meticulously and hurriedly transferring the supplies from one tree to another. Now, why one tree was so much more desirable than the other tree is a mystery. They looked to be pretty identical. And they were only about twenty-five feet apart. But these squirrels were clearly determined to live in one tree and not the other. Maybe the new tree had better schools—I don't know. But it was very captivating.

As we watched these squirrels build their neighborhood (there was a little community center and a drugstore going up as well), it struck me that there seemed to be a lot more squirrels around the yard lately. And, come to think of it, they seemed a lot *bolder* than they used to be. It used to be they would scurry away from us at the first sound of an opening door. No more. The other day one of them actually asked to use the phone.

And then I realized why: Bosco no longer chases them. He *sees* them—I can tell that he sees them; I watch his eyes as they track the squirrels running from here to there. He'll raise his head to watch them climb a tree, he'll swivel his neck to follow them as they round the corner of the house. He's not *un*interested, he's just not motivated to get up and go after them. Oh, he'll still eagerly chase anything thrown his way; a tennis ball or a ratty towel will entertain him like nobody's business. But the whole chasing squirrels thing seems to have run its course for him.

More and more, Bosco resembles the very syrup for which he was named: brown, sweet, and doesn't exactly move quickly. Both Bosco the syrup and Bosco the dog are very hard to get off of carpets, and when you do, both usually leave a stain. But I digress.

Sitting there that day, I tried to motivate him: "Bosco! Chase the squirrel!" (I meant it as a suggestion, not so much as a command, not that it matters.)

The dog does not move. Stretched out comfortably, his large brown head resting on his perfectly good front paws, he observes the growing population of hardworking, ambitious squirrels, and ignores them. And me.

"Taking the day off?" I ask.

Nothing makes a man look smaller than being sarcastic to a dog. And it has no effect on the dog. Suddenly, a squirrel dashes less than a foot from Bosco's nose and stops, terrified. This makes me happy. Bosco has not gotten that type of reaction in some time. I decide this must be a *new* squirrel, or maybe it was just very young when Bosco was last in the chasing business. Either way, the squirrel did not expect to see a ninety-pound carnivore within striking distance. For squirrels, this must be their worst nightmare; their version of driving off a cliff or showing up naked for a test they haven't studied for. Bosco looks at the squirrel with only mild interest. The squirrel darts away. Bosco yawns.

It didn't used to be this way. Squirrels used to be Bosco's main thing. Nothing could keep him from gamboling after them. Not that he ever caught one, though. In fairness, I don't know how hard he was really trying. He may have been in it just for the thrill of the chase. I always assumed it was like his version of golf. Like any committed amateur, he didn't seem to be bothered that nobody asked him to do it. Certainly nobody was ever going to pay him to do it. It didn't matter. He was doing something he loved. It got him out of the house. Fresh air, good exercise, no chance of getting hit by a car; and we inside the house got a nice break from having to scratch his ass. The squirrels didn't even seem to mind being chased much. All in all, it was good for everybody while it lasted.

For some reason, he's given it up.

At first we thought it could be his thyroid. Not for any reason in particular; never heard of a dog with a bad thyroid. But people we know complained about being sluggish themselves and went to the doctor and found out their thyroids were on the fritz.

We took Bosco to the vet. The dog's thyroid was fine. His weight was a little high, though. The vet suggested Bosco get more exercise.

"He used to love chasing squirrels," I offered. "Now it leaves him cold." The vet suggested Bosco might be bored with it. I said I found that hard to believe. The vet asked why. Did I think there was something especially *interesting* about chasing squirrels? (I maintain she said it like she meant it to be insulting. And not to Bosco either.)

I admitted that while squirrels were not necessarily interesting to *me*, as I am not a dog, Bosco, for the longest time, couldn't get enough of them. "Unless squirrels have changed dramatically over the last few months, I presume they are just as interesting now as they were back when Bosco chased them," I said, matching the vet's tone rather nicely, I thought. Bosco just stared at us.

The truth is, I'm not sure Bosco *can* be bored. And not because he's such a deep thinker that he finds meaning in every little thing. I don't mean to be cruel, I'm just saying that, having lived with Bosco since he was a pup, having spent hours and hours with him, having watched him eat, sleep, and stare, I just don't think the intellectual curiosity is there.

Don't get me wrong; he's *smart*. I often marvel at what he can deduce. When I come down the stairs, he can tell—before I've indicated a thing—if we're going out to pick up the paper from the driveway or if I'm just crossing to the couch. (And, I'm convinced, he can tell which day is Sunday and, furthermore, what that means in terms of the heft of the newspaper we'll be retrieving that day.)

When you toss him a piece of food, he can ascertain—*midair*, mind you—if the morsel is something to be gobbled down in one chew-less gulp (cheese, for example) or something on which he'd prefer to pass (cucumbers are not a big favorite).

This is a smart dog. In fact, he's smarter even than he needs to be. We're not sheep herders, nobody needs him to sniff out explosives, and we're not planning on shooting him into space anytime soon. So the fact that's he's not Steve Jobs, or even Flipper, is fine with me. I just found the idea that he was suddenly intellectually understimulated a bit far-fetched.

SOME PEOPLE ASCRIBE great intellect to their dogs. They'll tell you about all the great things the dogs can do: bring a can of soda, respond to telemarketers, explain the movie with Leonardo DiCaprio and the three dreams going on at the same time—complex endeavors.

This is not our dog. Like most dog owners, I talk to Bosco a lot, but I don't expect him to answer, and not because he doesn't speak English. (Because I maintain he *does*.) It's because even if he could talk, I'm pretty sure Bosco would have nothing to say. Should they ever come up with a phone app to let your dog talk, I know exactly how the conversation would go.

"Bosco! Chase the squirrel!"

"Uh . . . no."

"Why not?"

"Why not what?"

Like a cocktail party with painfully difficult small talk.

"Crazy weather, huh, Bosco?"

"Uh . . . okay."

"No, I mean, because, you know . . . it's been so hot."

"Uh . . . outside, you mean?"

"DOGS ARE NOT DIFFERENT than humans," the vet tells me
unnecessarily, clearly spoiling for a confrontation. "They like variety."

I assured the doctor that Bosco is *indeed* no different than
humans, in that he *hates* variety. This is a dog that does the same
thing the same way every single day; eats the same food, pees and
poops at the same time, at the same locations. He's like a big brown
clock: reliable, predictable—though furry. My point being: *variety*
is not what Bosco does.

"And *yet* you yourself say he no longer chases squirrels," the vet
said. (Her meeting my "indeed" with an even more snide "yet" was
not lost on me.) "Maybe if you varied his routine and played with
him more, he might enjoy the stimulation."

That comment was uncalled for, I thought. It was bad enough
that I felt inadequate as my *children's* father; did I need this lady to
make me feel inadequate as a dog dad too?

No man loves dogs more than I. If I loved them any more, it
would likely be frowned upon. But unlike a lot of other people, I
like dogs for what they are, not what I imagine them to be. Dogs
offer wonderful gifts. For many people, they're all the family they
need. For many others, they can be a gateway drug to having your
own kids; you start with a puppy, and before you know it, you're
hooked, and step up to raising little *humans*.

But human critters change. Infants become toddlers, who start
walking and talking and questioning your authority, and ultimately
move out.

Dogs don't do that. A dog stays a dog. That's what I love about Bosco. There's not that much room for improvement. Sure, if I were so inclined, I could probably teach him to shake hands or roll over, but he's never going to learn, for example, *irony*. Change is not what he does. Unconditional tolerance of humans? Of that, Bosco has an endless supply.

THE TRUTH IS, the vet wasn't wrong; I'm not a good pet dad. I used to be. Before we had kids (and I'm not blaming them), I was all over the dog. I walked him till he was exhausted; I petted him down to bare skin—there wasn't much I wouldn't do. I worried about his food, the luster of his coat, whether his livery pink nose was spotty enough, or maybe *too* spotty. My wife and I would debate whether it was cruel to clip all his paw-nails. Wouldn't it be more humane to leave one or two long in case he needed to scratch?

But with two kids, I just no longer have what it takes. There's just not that much concern, patience, or time left over in me. I'm sure if we were to have another child, I would find it within me to muster what's needed. But as it is, this is it. This is the full extension of all I can do. Deep inside, I know my dog understands this. And forgives.

Bosco remains a part of our family, just—I'm sorry to say—not the most important part anymore. Our boys sometimes forget to feed him. They're not beyond taking him for granted sometimes. See, they were *born* into having a dog. They never got a chance to *want* a dog, never had to beg their parents to get them a dog. There was no red ribbon around the gangly puppy's neck on their birthday. Bosco, like my wife and me, has always been a fact of their life. So I can't really blame them.

To be honest, I too also forget to feed him sometimes. Because he's almost the exact same shade as our carpet, I have occasionally and accidentally stepped on him. Because he's also the same shade as one of our couches, I have also occasionally laid upon him. Accidentally, and only briefly, but it happens. I feel terrible about it when it does, but Bosco, true to his nature, never gets upset.

"Uh . . . dude . . . ?"

"Oh, Bosco! I'm so sorry! I didn't see you there!"

"I'll move."

I feel bad for Bosco sometimes. The least demanding, most accepting, most even-keeled member of the family receives, for the most part, the least of our attention. He thrives on our scraps—scraps of time, scraps of contact, scraps of food. Like the best of us, like the kind and sainted, Bosco accepts what we have to give him without complaint.

We probably don't deserve such a good dog. I can only imagine what Bosco's friends must think of us. I bet they tell Bosco he could do better, that he ought to leave us. I can't really argue with them. But he works through it. I'm just glad he has someone to talk to.

AFTER WE COME HOME from the vet, I give Bosco an extra portion of dog food. And a muffin. And a little piece of steak. We sit out in the backyard. I watch him watch-but-not-chase squirrels. The squirrels scurry to and fro, building their mini-city. We sit there, enthralled. I wonder out loud if the influx of squirrels means some other group will be moving out. Perhaps the gophers. Bosco shrugs. He doesn't know either.

It's moments like this that make me proud to be his father.

Take My Kid.
Please.

OUR NEIGHBORHOOD HAS A TERRIFIC PUBLIC ELEMEN-tary school. So good, in fact, that when you enroll, the district literally sends an investigator to your house to confirm that you indeed live where you say you do; people outside the area have been known to lie about living here just so their kids can go to this school.

Fortunately, we didn't have to lie. We lucked out, living in the correct square-mile area. We sent both our boys to the school, and they loved it—and even shared many of the same teachers. It was a great experience.

But as our younger son was about to graduate—the school only goes to fifth grade—we had a big decision to make as to where he would go next. The public *middle* school of our particular district was not as stellar as the elementary school. So, as much as we were initially against the idea, we treaded into the murky world of apply-ing to private schools.

This is an exhausting and dispiriting journey for which I was wholly unprepared. The amount of planning and plotting and positioning and paperwork that goes into applying to private schools is staggering. And unsettling. Once you enter the arena, you are not only a stranger in a strange land, scavenging for mor-sels of information and access, but the jungle mentality perme-ates your every move. Other families—only days earlier your dear friends—are now the enemy, as they too plot to grab one of the precious few available openings. (Sometimes these enemies can throw you off balance with a disarming display of benevolence and shared information. "You know, if you get the applications in before next Monday, you get called in for the interview sooner, which increases your chances of admission." Sure, it's helpful. But don't let your guard down; there are still only so many spots available, and if their kid gets in, that's one less chance for your kid. Remember that!)

STEP ONE. Determine which schools you want to apply to. This will be the last time you feel remotely like you have the upper hand, because the moment that application is in, the tables turn and you are at the beck and call of the admissions board, and for the sake of your children's future, you will shamelessly jump through any and all hoops asked of you by these people.

Step Two. Fill out the absurdly intricate application packets they send you, with all the idiosyncrasies of their particular admissions process—which can vary immensely, but all involve a labyrinth of forms, questionnaires, and requests for *more* forms and questionnaires and records from previous schools, the execution of which could be so easily mishandled, presenting you a myriad of ways to drop the ball and prevent your child from advancing his or her education—the one your child would have gotten had you not misread Form 17A, misplaced Request for Transcript 24, or had you seen the part where they ask for the kid to submit an original haiku.

. . .

AN IRONIC TWIST of the whole ordeal is that while, theoretically, nothing could be more unifying for a mother and father than their joint attempt to advance their child's cause, in reality, nothing could be more stressful or chisel away more relentlessly at the foundation of an otherwise vibrant family. There were many moments during the application process when my wife and I were genuinely ready to walk away from the whole thing—the school, the marriage, and the will to live . . . *Everything.*

What was most jolting—and what I was least prepared for—was realizing that we were, for the first time, presenting our child for the approval of others. *We* know our children are extraordinary; an objective third party, however, might be . . . objective. This would not work in our favor. It becomes, therefore, our job to shine our children up and polish them, repackage and re-brand them before taking them to market—all in the hopes that they will meet with the approval of people we have never even met but already strongly dislike.

Filling out those forms is an intensely sobering and emotion-ally draining experience. I remember vacillating between deep pools of insecurity and abject resentment. On the one hand, we worried that we had utterly failed as parents and set our children on a path to almost certain failure. (Nobody wants their kids judged unfairly, but I wasn't that keen on having them judged *fairly* ei-ther.)

And at the same time, I was offended at the insensitivity and audacity of their questions.

"How would you describe your child's intellectual interests?"

I could try to impress: "He's just finished reading all of Marcel Proust."

Or I could be honest. "He's *ten*! He doesn't have any!"

Another bad question: "How does your child respond to direction?"

I chortled. "Are you kidding? He *hates* it. I mean, he's not a fire-starter or anything, but he's not what you'd call a *big fan* of authority. A good kid, don't get me wrong. But if there's a laugh to be had, particularly at the expense of any figure of authority, he's going to take the shot. In fact, he *lives* for it."

Upon reflection, I thought our son's chances might be better served if I perhaps massaged the truth more artfully.

"My son has never had a discipline problem. On the contrary; while he often engages in tomfoolery, if not outright hijinks, he virtually never gets caught, for which his mother and I are both enormously proud."

Or, as an alternative: "Our son recognizes authority. And like all good, patriotic Americans, he is often compelled to question it."

These were both shot down by my more levelheaded wife.

SOMETIMES, these application questions were shockingly ignorant and ill-conceived.

"What would you describe as your child's greatest academic weakness?"

Did they think I was going to tell them that? Did they really expect me to rat out my own kid? To "The Man"? What's wrong with these people?! I put down, "How about this: *You* take him, watch him for a couple of years, then *you* tell *me*. See how good *you* are at eye-balling the problem areas."

But I chickened out and deleted it.

Even when they invite you to be positive, the temptation to exaggerate is hard to resist.

"What are your child's academic strengths?"

Okay, glad you asked. "Our son's primary academic strength is his enormous untapped potential, much the way we as a society have yet to fully tap alternative, green energies, such as wind and solar power—which, by the way, our son shows tremendous interest in developing. He often speaks of his wish to save our nation from continued dependence on foreign oil."

Some applications are more encouraging than others. The nice ones give you ample room to expound upon your child's virtues in your own style, uncensored and unrestrained. "Describe in detail all the great things about your child."

Are you kidding? How much time do we have? Pull up a chair. Call home, tell them you're going to be late—we're going to be here awhile.

And then I started babbling on for pages about the virtues of my child.

"Oh, well . . . he's funny, he's bright, he's inquisitive, he's intuitive, he's got a killer smile, he's sweet . . . Why, one time, we were at our friend's house, and he saw this little turtle who was stuck in a—"

"Um, honey," my wife wisely interrupted. "It's a *school,* not your mother we're trying to impress here."

"Got ya," I acknowledged sheepishly. "Sorry. Got a little carried away."

I was appreciative, though, of the schools that were more diplomatic and nurturing in the wording of their questions. Instead of, for example, asking you to spill the beans and "list your child's weaknesses," they might ask, "In what areas of your child's education do you see the most opportunity for improvement?" Well, that's different. Who could be against their child improving? So I begin to list:

"Well, he doesn't always pay attention, his work habits are shabby, frankly. He never studies an iota more than legally required . . ."

"You really want to tell them all that?" my wife asks.

"Okay, how about this?" I say, pitching another angle—the "Truthful But Still Sucking Up" approach:

"He does very well in school when he tries, manages to do okay when he *doesn't* try, and he could do even better if he tried harder at your fine school."

This was shot down as well.

What we came to learn, with a bit of practice, was that with just the right terminology and turn of phrase, every "opportunity for growth" can be neatly spun into an incontrovertible "positive." For example, "He gets easily bored" becomes "He really blossoms when actively engaged." How about that, huh?

"Hates homework and tends to stare into space" transforms into "Learns as much from interpersonal activity and the world around him as he would from conventional texts." See what I did there?

"Once kicked a kid for looking at him funny" becomes "A respected leader of his peers."

I'm telling you: Once you get the hang of it, it's a cinch. Just a dollop of creative writing and a pinch of sheer linguistic daring, and suddenly your kid looks like exactly the kind of kid they'd be crazy not to take.

"HE MIGHT NOT GET ACCEPTED," my wife felt obliged to point out, seriously dampening my fledgling optimism.

Honestly, that had never even occurred to me—the idea that in the end, some school might not welcome him. I mean, yes, I understand it's a competitive field, but with our newly sparkling résumé-writing skills, and with his natural charm and killer smile, how could they *not* take him?

"You're kidding, right?" my wife said to me, holding her head cocked at that special angle that is her encouragement for others to think harder and remember. I had, in fact, totally forgotten that we already went through this exact thing with our older son—only five years earlier. I think I blocked out the memory.

In fact, that first go-round was, in some ways, even more excruciating, because our older son had specific challenges that made the choice of middle school that much more critical. We did extensive research and cherry-picked a few very specific, very specialized schools that we thought would be best for him. When they each, for various reasons, turned us down, I think I transitioned from "Ouch" to "The hell with them" so instantly and thoroughly that I now couldn't even recall the horror of it all. (The human spirit can be impressively self-sustaining sometimes.)

In our older son's case, we elected to homeschool him for a while, which was great until he eventually—and understandably—decided he would prefer to attend school with other kids, especially other kids who were *girls*, which was not something we offered in our home academy.

We have since found a terrific school for him where he thrives magnificently. (And while I'm not proud of this, not a day goes by that I don't think about the schools that rejected us and wish them—if not *ill*—at least a severe case of *painful remorse* for having passed over the opportunity to spend time with our son.)

Now, a scant few years down the road, here we were—doing it again. I decided that I would learn from the first experience and fortify myself with the knowledge that, come what may, we would prevail. Everything works out in the end. But let's at least give it our best shot!

So into the cold waters we plunged. We determined to do everything possible to get our ten-year-old accepted to the schools of our choice; we enrolled him in a four-month preparatory course, hoping to maximize his performance on the grueling standardized test they use to weed out your children. We gathered his transcripts, asked for letters of recommendation, wrote the essays, *re-wrote* the essays, had our son write his own mandatory self-evaluating essays ... We did everything to the very best of our abilities and were starting to feel pretty darn good about the whole thing.

The morning of the foreboding three-hour standardized test, as he reluctantly put on his shoes and packed his pencils and erasable pens and scratch paper and snacks, my sweet (and normally unflappable) ten-year-old quietly let fly his simple but deeply seated fear.

"What if they don't accept me?"

Oh, how I hated these people! Why would they design a system that causes this perfectly confident, wonderful child to feel this kind of self-doubt?

Though, deep inside, I knew it wasn't really their fault. This is what life is. To be alive means you're going to grow, you're going to move forward. And that will necessarily involve making an effort. *Trying,* which by definition involves, if not failure, then at least the *risk* of failure. And rejection, and heartbreak. Ain't no way around it.

But the pain of your children being rejected—and witnessing *them* experience that rejection—is as brutal a part of parenting as there is. It taps into every skill set and deep well of character strength you hope you have. You ache to not only soothe their bruised hearts, but in the process, hopefully, also shed some light on the ways of the world that might make the next inevitable disappointment easier to swallow.

More than anything, it was his simple use of the word "accept" that killed me. It was the very word we had bandied about for months—"Hope they *accept* us." "Think they'll *accept* us?" "When do they let us know if they *accept* us or not?" "The idiots better *accept* us!" and so on.

But when my son said it, it sounded so painfully openhearted and vulnerable. "What if they don't accept me?"

I remembered a time when he had asked the same thing about *me*. I had just written a script I was really excited about and submitted it to some studios to see what "they" had to say. Its fate was no longer in my control. And it is not fun having the fate of something precious to you in the hands of others.

One day the phone rang and my son—knowing how eager I was to get the "yes" call—came into the room and stood by me, listening to my end of the conversation, trying to read my expressions for a clue. Finally, ever hopeful, fingers to his mouth in excited anticipation, he whispered, "So? Did they accept you?"

Broke my heart. That he saw it so clearly and honestly. Yes, nobody else's opinions should ever impact so decisively anyone else's sense of self-worth. But that's how it always seems to play out; we feel "accepted" or "not accepted." It's really that simple.

When my young son wondered if he'd be accepted to these schools, it was more than getting admitted to them he was fretting about; it was the universal acceptance of *him*. The very being of who he was. What would he do if they rejected *him*? he wondered.

I assured him that first of all, I was more than confident he would do great on the test. Which was true; he's a smart kid. But even if he didn't do as well as he hoped, the test was only a *part* of what they looked at. They also considered his grades at school (all pretty good), his various activities (he was pretty darn active), his interests (he was very interested), and most importantly—*himself.* The sparkling, shining, wonderful *him*. When they sat with him for the obligatory interview, how could they not be impressed with what a gem of a guy he is? Why would they want to have a school without him in it?

"They might," he offered. "They might not accept me."

I had nothing else I could say. "That's true," I said. "They might not."

Unfortunately, part of being a parent involves explaining things to your kids that you yourself don't understand. Best I could do, I decided, was to try to put things in perspective for him: enjoy when the judgments are in your favor, I suggested, and accept when they are not, but never put your faith in them entirely, because they are subjective, mysterious, and often meaningless things. No judgment can tell you who you are or what you can be, and no judgment is final as long as we are alive and able to put ourselves out there again and again.

This either made sense to him, or he was so over the whole thing that he pretended it did. Either way, we were done talking about it.

STEP THREE: The interview.

We go visit the first of the schools to which we've applied (our top choice, actually) for our Family Interview. (Isn't that nice—how they make it Fun for the Whole Family!) But I convinced myself that barring anything extreme—like my punching the director of admissions in the nose, or accidentally (or deliberately) besmirching their carpets—our kid was going to sink or swim on *his* merits alone.

We show up on time and properly dressed—our son having consented to long pants, a clean shirt, and a perfunctory combing of his hair, but nothing so out of the ordinary that he would feel in any way not "himself."

They come to call him for his one-on-one with the director. Mom and Dad wait outside—our interview will follow his.

As he heads away and down the hall, he exudes not only his usual confidence and sparkle, but a freshly minted surge of independence. He avoids even making eye contact with us, assuming full responsibility on his own shoulders. He has accepted that he will make it or *not* make it entirely by virtue of what he and he alone can do. His mother and I do a reasonable job of containing our tears of pride and sniffles of wonderment (which, as you may recall, was also the name of the band in the late sixties most famous for their Top 40 hit, "Dream Tissue").

Thirty minutes later, our son and the director emerge from their closed-door meeting. The poker-faced ten-year-old reveals nothing as he is guided to a work-desk for further "evaluation." The school director invites us into the same room where he just sat with our son. He closes the door.

We make some small talk, and in very short order he smiles and can barely contain himself when he confides that our son is *exactly* the type of child they want in their school. Possibly the very *epitome* of what they're looking for. The clearly brilliant educator proceeds to list all the qualities that our son was able to manifest in their very first—and brief—encounter. "Well, obviously, your son is exceptionally bright. He's inquisitive, he's intuitive, he's courageous and spirited, he looks at things from a very fresh perspective . . ."

We could not have asked for a better outcome. We were thrilled—not to mention enormously relieved—that the worst of our fears would not come to pass; while he might not be accepted to *all* the schools he applied to, our son would at least not end up "school-less." He seemed all but guaranteed open-armed admission to this school. And, equally important: he would be spared the pain of being resoundingly rejected.

This was a perfect day.

As we walked through the school on our way out, we saw even more confirmation and validation. The kids that went to this school—as much as we could tell from peeks through classroom doors and their effervescent strides down the halls—seemed to all be happy, confident, well-adjusted young boys and girls. In fact, the boys who were about our son's age even all looked and dressed kind of like him. This seemed, indeed, to be a perfect match.

As we strutted victoriously toward our car, our only-moments-old sense of relief and confidence slowly began to give way to other, less healthy impulses. We each—my wife and I—independently started to wonder if perhaps this wasn't *too* close a match. Maybe this school wouldn't stretch our son as much as one of the other schools might.

"Maybe this school is too easy to get into," my wife whispered to me.

"I know," I whispered back. "I was just thinking the same thing."

It was shortly thereafter I made a very big decision: our children are not going to college—I can't go through this again.

Emotional Baggage vs. Luggage

—⁂—

I'M NOT A PARTICULARLY NERVOUS FLYER. I AM, HOW-ever, a nervous *packer*. I worry about not having enough stuff, too much stuff, the wrong stuff. ("Am I really going to need a sports jacket? What if I'm the only one there who doesn't have one? Or the only one who *does* have one, and others mock me just for packing it?")

Then of course there's the anxiety that the stuff you ultimately pack may not even make it to wherever you're going. Will my stuff get lost or mangled? The idea that I myself could get lost or mangled is not a concern, but the possibility of my pants and pajamas going through that kind of trauma rattles me to the core.

Packing for the whole family, this anxiety is multiplied a hundredfold. Forget *me*—now it's "Do my *children* have the right clothes? Will they be warm enough? Will they be *too* warm? Will they look like slobs? Will they look *too* well dressed? Do they have enough things to amuse them? Do they have *too many* things to amuse them?" It's downright exhausting—and we haven't left the house yet.

NOT LONG AGO, we went on vacation, the whole family. We got to the airport, checked our bags, and went to wait for our flight. Within minutes, there was an announcement, paging my son.

"Hmm . . . that's odd," I thought. My son looked at me, a bit tickled and a bit nervous. He had never heard his name blared out loud in a public place like that. Could it be a mistake? I wondered. Is there possibly someone else with his name at this airport at this moment and they are actually paging *him*? Unlikely. Maybe it is a prank. As it happened, his birthday was the next day, so I decided that the airlines must have noticed his date of birth when we checked in and were going to make a little bit of a big deal, give him a special cookie or something.

So we headed over to the counter, where the nice airline lady was on the phone, indeed discussing my son, and his luggage. Quickly calculating the possibilities, I decided the problem must be his video games. They'd triggered some security sensor; too many electromagnetic digital gigabytes could potentially knock out the plane's navigation system. Or perhaps the actual content of the game was so violent that even packed away inside his suitcase, the very idea of it was deemed a threat to public safety. So as to not make him any more nervous, my wife and I told our little guy to go relax—we'd deal with it.

It was soon explained to us that, in fact, his bag had somehow gotten caught in the rollers of the conveyer belt while it was being loaded onto the plane and ripped wide open. Nothing was lost, the agent assured us; just the bag was damaged. They had since taped it securely shut and, of course, would reimburse us for a replacement. This call to the desk was, apparently, merely a courtesy "heads-up" so we wouldn't be alarmed upon arriving at our destination. All in all, a very nice handling of a minor, albeit unpleasant mishap.

But my heart sank for the little guy. First of all, he had just gotten the suitcase—the first of his very own. It was a rite of passage for him; he was very proud of it. But also, this was a specific nightmare I have always feared—the ripped-open luggage at the airport. We've all seen the poor guy whose bag implodes in transit, and who stands there at the baggage carousel pathetically watching his clothes pour down. You do not want to be *that* guy. It's almost too painful a humiliation to consider: all your personal effects violated and on pathetic parade for public viewing. I always look away; it seems the charitable thing to do. Give the guy a little space to gather his underwear with a modicum of dignity.

And now, my sweet little boy *was* that guy. My wife and I went to tell him the bad news. As is often the case in these matters, we had different ideas about how to handle it. I suggested we wait; why should he spend the next several hours upset about his dead suitcase? I argued. We could tell him when we landed; let him live in innocence a few more hours. My wife—an ardent proponent of Full Disclosure All the Time—disagreed. She thought our son should know everything that we knew. Not feeling particularly strongly about it, I acquiesced.

We told him about the bag, and to my great surprise, he was totally fine with it. Eerily flippant, actually. I believe his exact words were "Okay, whatever." I couldn't have been prouder. Truly. For a kid who *loves* his things, he handled the news remarkably well. (Maybe because the only thing he cared about—his video games— were, as it turns out, safely in his carry-on.) But, no matter. I was impressed and inspired; he had shown me a thing or two about retaining equilibrium in the face of life's little bumps.

HOURS LATER, we landed and went to collect our bags, prepared for the worst. His bag comes around and, surprise of surprises, it doesn't look bad at all. Can't even see the tape. Or the rip. Maybe they got it wrong and it was some other poor sap whose bag got shredded.

It was. *My* bag came down next. Apparently, we had somehow put *his* name on *my* bag, and vice versa. When I saw my bag spit out of the luggage chute, my stomach clenched. It looked like a toy left too long in the gorilla cage, on the day the gorilla had a playdate with a shark. And a monsoon. And a civic uprising. Ripped to pieces it was, my not inexpensive, supposedly damage-proof feat of technological engineering. Hours earlier, when I thought it was my son's bag that had been destroyed, I think I even said to my wife, "I hate that this happened to him! I wish it could have been *my* suitcase instead." I can't believe that out of all the wishes I've thrown out there over the years, *this* is the one I'm granted. (And I didn't even really mean it.)

Thankfully, the airline pros had done a very thorough job of taping the suitcase up, shrink-wrapping the thing entirely in industrial-strength cellophane, so at least the individual items weren't streaming down one at a time—which would have, frankly, put me in the hospital. All the bag's contents were securely cellophaned up.

But it was *see-through* cellophane, so everything was still clearly visible, frozen in awkward, ugly suspension. Like pathetic fossils captured at the moment of their death, sealed for eternity, faces screaming against the outer surface, straining desperately to break through. Oh, the stories they longed to tell! ("The ground shook, and the gods' anger rained down upon us!") Except, instead of ancient Greek shepherds, this was my underwear. And socks. And pajamas.

My wife, bless her heart, knows me well enough to know that nothing in the world could make me less happy than what was in fact happening. She calmly took charge, suggesting I go wait on the side while she gathered the butchered luggage. I waited at a safe distance, shielding my eyes. It was like childbirth; the woman knows what to do, and the father (in this case, the father of *luggage*) has only to get out of the way and wait for the messy part to be over with.

I'M NOT SURE when this particular aversion of mine developed—the fear of a publicly violated suitcase. I'm not suggesting anybody *enjoys* it, but I remember having this specific phobia even as a kid. And becoming an adult has done nothing to alleviate the anxiety. Nor has having been on TV. Fittingly, I have exactly the kind of recognition that's small enough to not do me any good, but big enough to draw attention when I wouldn't want it. I would never count on getting a good table at a crowded restaurant, but I'm pretty confident that if my underpants were to be scattered about Delta Airlines Carousel 5, the video would find its way onto YouTube. ("Former TV Funny Boy wears briefs! And ratty ones, too!")

I suppose I should take solace in the fact that the contents were, in fact, perfectly mundane and universal. *Everyone* has socks, underwear, and a toothbrush. It would have been a lot more embarrassing if I'd been packing, say, sex toys. Or cheese. Or a severed human head. I had *normal* stuff; exactly what ten out of ten people have in *their* bags. So why, then, should it be so crippling to have it be seen? It's like the proverbial tree; if you trip and fall in the forest and no one sees, is it still embarrassing? Well, yeah, but . . . who cares? It's a *private* failure; in that case, failure to walk without falling down. But having your bag ripped apart in an airport is a *public* failure. Failure to . . . well, to avoid being the poor son of a bitch that that stuff happens to.

I don't understand why it is we're so embarrassed by those very things that, in fact, happen to everyone. You would think such misfortunes would serve to bring us closer; celebrations of our common, flawed humanity.

But it doesn't work that way. Think of any public scandal: the elected official caught with his pants down; the celebrity fighting unattractively with a loved one; the rock star spotted picking his nose at a stoplight . . . Nothing each of us hasn't done, or couldn't, without much imagination, picture ourselves doing. You'd think that as a group, we'd embrace these poor fallen brothers and sisters all the more at these moments. Feel their pain. But we don't. We go the other way; we beat them into submission with their unfortunate falls from grace. And why? Because we're so happy it's *them* and not *us*. We get giddy and rambunctious with nervous relief. All the shouting, pointing, ridiculing, and memorializing is just our attempt to push further away the possibility of it ever happening to *us*.

Embarrassment, I've decided, is a factor of age. My kids get embarrassed at the drop of a hat—usually by me. (Which is ironic, because I vividly remember every single thing my parents did that embarrassed me, and swore even as a child that I would not repeat those indignities with my own children. But I do, with shocking regularity.)

Kids still think they're the first ones to ever experience embarrassment. And why wouldn't they? They're new here. They haven't yet learned that everything happens to everyone.

Old guys, on the other hand, don't care anymore. And I'm not talking about an unflattering cartoon caricature of old guys—addle-brained incontinents who spend their days talking to cats. I'm talking about dignified men—friends of mine in their eighties who have attained every measure of success in their fields. These guys don't "do" embarrassment; they're beyond it. So what happens between nine and eighty-nine that makes that happen? (Relax. I'll try to answer; you just sit there.)

I think that all our lives, we feel the pull of two conflicting forces: the desire to blend in and the desire to stand out. (And by "stand out," I mean standing out by virtue of an *accomplishment*; something of our own choosing. As opposed to standing out because a trail of toilet paper is stuck to your shoe and everyone sees but you. That's different. And not at all the goal here.)

Furthermore, we never want *too much* of either. We want just the right amount of blending in and standing out.

You have to start with the blending in; then you can aspire to stand out. But sometimes, in the effort to stand out, you can fail. And then you wish you could just blend in. Until you tire of blending in, and then start dreaming again of standing out.

As a kid, I was not a particularly great athlete. Playing baseball, for example, going 0 for 4 was considered a good day. (A bad day was going 0 for 4 and getting hurt.) I knew I wasn't likely to make the spectacular catch or hit the walk-off grand slam. I just wanted to get on base once in a while, and not let a ball go through my legs. That's all. I prayed just to not conspicuously *fail*. (The praying rarely worked, by the way.)

Now. Had I in fact gotten on base with regularity, and fielded everything that came my way, I would have been able to cross that wish off the list, and most likely I would've gotten greedy and upped the ante; I would have wanted that walk-off home run. I would have tried to stand out. But that can only come with the confidence of having already blended in.

Over the years, I've managed to blend in, by and large. I've even had the good fortune to occasionally stand out for doing some things that have met with success. And as childhood drifts further into the distance, I begin to see what my older friends have learned, and what I try to teach my children: everything truly does happen to everyone. We *all* want to blend in, and we *all* want to stand out—for the right reasons. In fact, it's the universal fear of standing out from the crowd for the *wrong* reason that makes us a "crowd" in the first place, I believe. That's what unites us. We're *already* all blended in from the get-go. So run free and enjoy your life, I tell them. There's no reason for any of us to ever be embarrassed about anything.

Except having your underwear fall out at the airport. That's . . . that's just embarrassing.

Loyalty

I 'LL TELL YOU SOMETHING ABOUT MY WIFE THAT ONLY makes me admire and love her more: she can cut in line in front of people, and not only make it look like a good thing, she can make you feel bad for questioning it in the first place.

We were with the kids, in line for a museum. Freezing cold. Blustery winds. Lines around the block and then on to other blocks. The options were: (a) go home and try again some other time, or (b) go to the back of the line, which was so far away it was about the same size trip as going home.

We kind of slinked off, not having clearly decided either way, but when we got to the corner, my wife came up with a third option, called "Let's just get in line right *here!*"

A great idea—if you discounted the fact that this would be "cutting," thereby sticking it to the three thousand people already waiting in line behind you, who only *seemed* to not be there because the line picked up over there, across the street. So if you closed your eyes and tuned out the vitriolic taunts of the three thousand people who wanted to beat you to death, and shut off entirely your moral compass and sense of decency, then yeah, you could, conceivably, convince yourself that you had arrived at the legitimate end of the line.

Now, don't get me wrong; my moral compass is nothing if not flexible. And I certainly didn't want to stand out in arctic winds any longer than necessary. But I knew this was just *wrong*. (Also, the stares and threats and the colossal wave of ill will washing over us from all sides were impossible to ignore.)

I leaned in to confer with my wife.

"Honey, we can't cut in line."

She looked at me so oddly I thought maybe I had missed something obvious, like "Don't you remember the proclamation the mayor made yesterday granting us the right to do exactly this if we needed to?"

I started again to—gently and confidentially—voice my protest.

"Sweetie, I don't think we can—"

But again I got that look—this time a bit more intensely—that wordless glare that indignantly argued "What are you talking about? I'm not *cutting in line*."

Now, understand: This was coming from a sane person. An extremely intelligent woman, and—I feel compelled to reiterate here—a *good* person. Maybe the best I've ever known; an extraordinarily empathetic, caring woman. This is a woman who has reached out to some of the absolutely most hateful people you'd ever want to meet—people I had lobbied strenuously to jettison from our lives—and she has cared for them, brought them into our house, clothed and fed them, and never asked for so much as a thank-you. This is a woman who hates bullies, snobs, and liars, who detests pretense or anyone taking advantage of anyone else; the last person on earth who you could ever see cutting in line. And she wouldn't.

Except for the fact that she just *did*.

But in her mind, at that moment, she was convinced she had done nothing wrong. I couldn't tell you the particular path of logic she followed to get there, or the exact formula of denial she used to leap the many readily apparent hurdles of reality. I just knew that somewhere in the previous few moments, something had changed in her and she had gone "there." That place she goes sometimes from which I can't get her back until she decides on her own to return.

I know this is a place she goes only when it concerns her children. In this particular case, she was just doing what she felt she had to do to get her children out of the freezing cold—even if it meant partaking in an act that she herself, at any other time, would vociferously oppose.

I felt the need to illuminate.

"But, sweetie," I said, as tenderly as I could. "We actually *are* cutting in line." I smiled, trying to appeal to her higher angels, which I knew lived somewhere inside her, but were apparently staying in to avoid the cold.

The smile didn't work. She clenched her jaw slightly and looked straight through the very center of my eyes—another of her deep supply of silent signals, this one imploring me unequivocally to "just drop it." Fair enough. As she scooted our kids into the line, I fell in behind them, now a knowing and guilt-ridden accomplice.

Shortly later, as we all shuffled forward a few inches, I could feel on my neck the white-hot hatred of those behind us. Once or twice I turned around and shrugged apologetically, as if to say, "What are you going to do?"—hoping for some kindred spirit to assuage my guilt. Perhaps some other husband who, like me, knows what it's like to be caught in the crosscurrents of that which is right and that which your spouse has already committed you to and which you are powerless to abandon.

When I got no sympathy from anyone—and why should I have, really?—I was surprised to feel a shift inside me. The sense of embarrassment and self-conscious guilt gave way to something else: a defiant sense of allegiance. While yes, my wife may have fired that first shot and started this whole thing, I now felt honor-bound to stand and fight beside her and continue the battle she'd chosen, while our children huddled against our legs for warmth. (All so we could get into this museum, which, by the way, the kids would have been thrilled to skip entirely.)

But being a family involves being *loyal* to the family. And part of that loyalty—who are we kidding—*absolutely all* of that loyalty is about going along with family at the very times you'd like to cover your head and deny even knowing these people.

It's easy to go along with your wife and kids when they're being nice and sweet and reflecting well upon your family name. That's not loyalty; that's taking a free ride on the love train. That's basking in the warmth of their pleasing, pleasant ways. When my little guy plays drums in the school play and I tap every parent in the auditorium on the shoulder to say, "That's my boy!"—that's not loyalty. That's just me unable to control my bursting heart. When my big guy works on a presentation for class and then nails it perfectly in front of the whole school, and I see him beam with pride and self-confidence as he accepts the heartfelt applause of his peers, that's not loyalty that makes my face hurt from smiling so hard and trying not to cry at the same time. That's just a parental cookie. That's a treat you get once in a while—a reward for hanging in there.

Loyalty is when it's *not* so easy. When your kid is being whiny and rude, or trying out poop jokes on his grandmother and her friends, or entering a room full of company naked and holding a *Star Wars* Light Saber in a very special way—try applauding *then*. Stand up with pride then and tell everyone, "I'm with *him!*" *That's* loyalty.

You don't do it because you approve of the behavior. You do it because you're family. And loyalty is a small price to pay for all the good things they do, all the proud moments they give. And all the loyalty they send your way when you embarrass them by wearing that hat they begged you not to, or tell a story for the thousandth time and they listen anyway. Loyalty is what you do.

And my wife is nothing if not a *doer*. This is a get-it-done gal. And if her children are involved, it will most assuredly get done, and my heart goes out to anyone who—intentionally or not—gets in her way.

We were traveling a few years ago and checked in to our hotel later than we'd expected. By the time we got up to our rooms, the kids, much younger at the time, were hungry and tired. My wife called for room service.

"Sorry," they said. "We're closed."

My wife, very sweetly, convinced them that they were in fact *not* closed, because our boys were hungry. After a few volleys of parries and thrusts and artfully veiled threats, the poor guy relented.

"Fine. What would you like?"

This was when the boys ate only, maybe, two things, one of which was pasta.

"Sorry," said the still-not-getting-it room service fellow. "We don't *have* pasta."

Again, even more sweetly, my wife convinced him that a tip-top kitchen like theirs must surely have some pasta somewhere, even if it's not, as he reported, on the menu at this hour. "In fact," she offered, "if you want, I can come down and help you look, if that'd be easier for you."

Needless to say, she didn't have to go anywhere. Within minutes, the nice fellow was at our door with two steaming bowls of pasta for our very appreciative children. My wife gave him a gracious and heartfelt thank-you and he left looking not that much worse for the ordeal. In fact, he seemed rather pleased with himself. It was a win-win situation.

This ferocious lioness instinct may have always been part of my wife's personality, I'm not sure. I do know it was already intact and fully operational from the instant she first became a mother.

When our older son was born, he was kept in the hospital for several months, fighting his way forward day by day. But he didn't do it alone. My wife was there at his side, vigilant, proactive, and tireless. I was there too—when I wasn't "busy" at work—a regretful ordering of priorities that, while justifiable, embarrasses me to this day.

My wife, though, never left that hospital room. She had her eyes on everyone who came to his bed, and her eyes out for the others who *should* have come but were momentarily elsewhere. She spent every waking moment making sure our son had the best care, the best treatment, and the best chance. She never left; her lion cub was sick. Nothing would take her away from fighting for him. Her loyalty was so strong, so fierce, it humbled me, almost frightened me. But it saved our son and made us a family.

So, if someday, while taking that very family to the museum or the zoo or a concert that's absurdly overcrowded, the mother of my children feels compelled to cut in line because she believes it's what her children need, am I going to complain? Yes—but quietly. And to myself.

And to all the people behind us in line—that day, and any day it may happen in the future—I sincerely apologize. It was wrong of us. It's just that . . . It's very . . . See, we're not really . . . She just . . .

You talk to her.

Currency

ONCE IN A WHILE I GET IT JUST RIGHT.

We're in the ocean, my younger son and I, and he's playing in the waves, being brave, or pretending to be brave. (Not that there's a difference; brave is brave, as far as I'm concerned.)

My little brown-haired seal of a son is having the time of his life, up to his chest in cool ocean water, jumping up to meet each new wave with palpable anticipation and joy. Except every once in a while there's a wave a bit larger than he'd like. I see him hesitate and steady himself for the inevitable, because in the ocean, there's no negotiating; that wave is coming whether you like it or not.

I stand nearby; close enough to grab him should he need grabbing, far enough away (and behind him) so he doesn't feel I'm cramping his style. As I watch him gauge each incoming wave with keenly focused consideration, I'm impressed—not to mention *relieved*; this is a kid who bounds through life with such seeming fearlessness, I am thrilled to see him, in fact, register fear when a small dose of fear is exactly what's called for.

Every third or fourth wave, I notice him turn ever so slightly to make sure I'm there. I am indeed. Happy to be there. No—much more than happy. *Ecstatic* to be there, enjoying such splendor with my son. Happy to see my child literally find his place in the universe. Watching him inch deeper and deeper into the world with all that I would hope he would bring: determination, exuberance, some caution, and the capacity to adjust as needed. My heart pulses with sheer, unending love.

I SOMETIMES WONDER if a child can ever be *too* loved. Probably not.

I know my children know they're loved. I'm not shy about telling them so in unedited, unrestrained, unconditional declarations. In fact, I once said—to this very same son—"Hey, did I ever tell you I love you?" (This was meant to be humorously rhetorical, since we both knew quite well I say it all the time.) His response? A slight rolling of the eyes and a perfectly annoyed "Yes, you *did*. Too much, frankly."

Boy, that made me laugh. I was very gratified that he had such an abundance of love in his life that he could comfortably afford to shoo away any intrusive excess. (I also, frankly, loved his use of the word "frankly." Not necessarily common sentence structure for a little kid.)

But his point was well taken; too many "I love you's" can be too much. (Still better than too *few*, but a good point nonetheless.) The problem with saying it too often is it starts to lose its impact. It becomes devalued. Like the Italian lira; when eight thousand of them only amount to one can of orange soda, each one seems to not be worth that much. Too many unfiltered expressions of adoration and it all becomes meaningless white noise.

So I've learned to contain myself. To hold back the number of "I love you's" I let fly in my kids' direction. Just like the Federal Reserve, sometimes you have to rein in and limit the supply of currency so as to retain its worth.

Looking at it for a moment from the other side of the coin, I know confidently that my children love *me*, but I wouldn't necessarily want

to be peppered with verbal reminders from them either. Sure it's
sweet, and a well-timed affirmation like that can sustain an emo-
tionally deprived parent for months.

But to be honest, when my kids do, on the rare occasion, let
forth an "I love you, Daddy," I'm suspicious. I figure they either
want something, broke something, or are saying it because it's easier
than saying what's really on their mind—like "There's something
hanging out of your nose," or "I can't believe you just called that
guy Ed; his name is *Justin*. You're just wrong so often."

And even if none of the above were the case—even if they said
"I love you" sincerely, unsolicited, and free of any ulterior motive—
well . . . it could still be too much because I don't always know what
to do with that much tenderness at one time. It can be hard to hold.

Fortunately, children have other currencies of affection besides
straightforward verbal declaratives. When they come over and
show you what they've made, when they repeat something they've
heard that tickled them, when they reference something you said to
them months earlier, when they call you something silly or when
they grab your head and twist and poke a finger into your face and
make horrendously rude noises—those are all universally accepted
and highly valued currencies of love. I've come to realize that none
of these are any less negotiable a currency than "I love you," and in
many ways they're better, because they're less predictable, less
pedestrian, less "on the money." Just as with gift giving, sometimes
"cash" is just tacky; better to go the unexpected route.

SO ON THIS BRILLIANT DAY at the beach, I marveled at the sight
of my son frolicking in the water, and rather than try to impress
upon him how great it was to watch him, or how unbelievably,

deeply, irrevocably, and incessantly loved he is, or even to remind him that I was there if he needed help, I contained myself. I don't do containment well. Or easily. But this time, I did. I said nothing—just enjoyed the moment and gave him his space.

And then a funny thing happened. A really big wave was heading in, and my fearless son—very subtly and without a sound—reached back for me. With no ceremony or self-consciousness, he took my arm, and then the other, and wrapped them around his waist like a seat belt. He placed his hands on my forearms and pushed down a little—testing the strength of his emergency landing system. He leaned back into me for security, and the wave came. It broke over us, tossing us both up and off balance—and then lowered us back to standing. No harm done. He laughed, and then—again, with no fanfare and no words exchanged—my brave son let go of my arms, fixed his eyes on the next wave, and stood to meet it. On his own.

That event—a span of maybe ten seconds—remains among the most fulfilling experiences of my life. My son needed me, and knew without looking that I'd be there for him.

For my part, I was thrilled to have come through. I was able to provide exactly what he needed; to be his safe harbor, the lifeboat, silently there if called upon.

If he gets to pretend he's always brave, then I get to pretend too. I get to pretend that this is how it will always be; that I'll be there for him forever, in and out of the ocean, ready to let him wrap himself up in me until the wave passes.

And all of this happened without a word exchanged. I didn't have to say anything or do anything. I had only to be there.

Like I say: once in a while I get it just right.

The Empty
Nest

D URING THE LAST EARTHQUAKE, THE ELECTRICITY
went out in our house. Actually, it may not have been an earthquake. It could have just been high winds. Or a guy working on the
cable TV. Or a coyote playing games, it's hard to tell; unless a me-
teor slams specifically into your house, you never know exactly
why the power goes out. It just does.

Unlike most people, I kind of like when the power goes out. As
a responsible person who pays his electric bills, and who is also in
no way handy around the house and could therefore never do anything with wires that might *cause* an outage, I enjoy basking in the
knowledge that if the power does go out, it couldn't possibly be my
fault. That right there is a nice treat.

To me, the power going out is like a free, safe holiday. Sure, if I
was hooked up to an iron lung, I might feel differently. But as emer-
gencies go, the power going out is the best. Beats the heck out of a
tsunami or a military insurrection.

I like how quiet things get when there's no power. The *whir* of
the air-conditioner, the soft gurgle of the water heater, the barely
perceptible *zizzzing* of all your big and little appliances—it all just
stops. Suddenly your house is just your house: four walls and a roof
holding in you and your family, and air. It's a refreshingly existential experience. All you have is each other. (And the sound of ice
cream melting in your freezer.) You have nothing to do but talk,

and see each other anew. You can imagine what it must have been like before all our devices stole our attention. You can almost hear everything sighing, enjoying a much needed moment to breathe.

And then, as it always does, the power comes back. The *whirring* and *zizzzing* begins again, and life returns to normal. But for an instant, as everything kicks back into gear, I catch myself wishing the power had stayed off just a little longer. Because it's in those quiet moments that I realize that what makes the house zizzz isn't the electricity or all the machines and gizmos we clutter our days with. It's the people inside the house. It's the ones you love that make your house hum.

And it was with this recognition that I steeled myself for the day last summer when both my boys were going away to summer camp for the first time, leaving my wife and me alone with nothing but four walls, a roof, and a symphony of electric humming and zinging. I dreaded the silence.

EVER HEARD THE CLICHÉ "A home without the sounds of children is just a house"? Well, to that I would like to say: "Yes, but it sure is a nice place to *read the friggin' newspaper in peace and quiet!*" It sure is a lovely opportunity to have a conversation without forty-seven interruptions. To eat a meal without someone discovering new ways to make milk disgusting. To not jump to mop up spilled juice. To not cringe at the sound of someone small crashing into something hard and unyielding. To not have to threateningly count backward from three to get the TV turned off. To not bark the words "He asked you to stop, so just stop!" To not have to answer questions you either don't know the answer to or can't answer because it will lead to a hundred more questions you don't feel like answering . . . The whole thing is just a delightful change of pace.

This surprised me, I have to say. I couldn't believe the unabashed glee with which my wife and I skipped about the house; the thrill of finding ourselves alone for the first time in . . . seemingly forever.

And we had charted out some pretty ambitious plans for ourselves. We were going to eat *whatever* we wanted *whenever* we wanted. We would watch every show we had recorded but never managed to actually see. We were going to prance naked in parts of the house heretofore unaccustomed to our nakedness. A second honeymoon is what we had here. And much more deserved than the first one, really, because what were we running away from back then? A few consecutive meals with parents and friends? An awaiting pile of obligatory thank-you notes? The returning of a few rented tuxedos? That was nothing. *This* honeymoon was deserved. After months on end of school, homework, scheduling appointments, playdates, pickups, drop-offs . . . the zizzz and whir of life, we'd *earned* this. The chance to be an actual loving couple for a few blessed weeks.

So with a quick check of the email to see that the kids arrived safely at camp, we were off. Mom and Dad's first time at Camp "How Great Is This?" was under way.

Admittedly, it took a little getting used to. It was an odd sensation, for example, to realize we didn't have to constantly check the time. It didn't matter that it was after nine; no one had to get to bed. We didn't have to talk in code or lower our voices to volumes audible only to each other and certain breeds of dogs; there was no one else there. We could do whatever we wanted. Crazy things. Like go out for a coffee and come back whenever we felt like it! It was a New World, I tell you. And I liked it.

Till around ten-fifteen. Then it felt really odd. The quiet was unsettling. As we headed upstairs to go to bed (so much for the late nights of reckless abandon we had planned), I went through my nightly lock-down ritual: I checked the doors, checked the windows, and walked by the boys' rooms. That's when it hit me. Not that they weren't in the rooms—I knew that. Not even that I missed them; I'd anticipated that, and even believe that missing the ones you love is not such a terrible thing once in a while. What rocked me completely was realizing that this thing I do every night— stopping by their rooms to make sure they're safe and sound—was clearly more for *me* than for *them*.

Truth be told, on any given night, there's very little that can go wrong between the time they head up for bed and the time they get *into* bed. That end-of-day sign-off, I only now realized, was for *my* benefit. It's what made me feel like a father. It wasn't the *only* thing, of course, but it was a crucial one. It gave me a sense of purpose. Maybe the last thing they saw before they closed their eyes didn't really have to be me, but it filled my heart to think so. I hadn't realized how completely my identity was defined by being the father of my kids. And with no kids around to actually father, what was I? Just a guy shutting off lights and sticking my head into empty rooms.

I loped pathetically to the bedroom to commiserate with my wife. We noted the odd silence. Not that our kids are particularly noisy at this time of night, being sound asleep and all. But still, the fact that they were now being silent somewhere other than across the hall made me sad. And envious. I resented whatever idiot sixteen-year-old counselor it was that got to sleep in the same bunk with them. I was bitter that he didn't even appreciate what he had there. I was like a dumped lover who spends an unhealthy amount of time picturing the ex with the new guy. "He'll never love you like I love you."

THE DAYS WORE ON. Like Papillon, I took to making *X*s on the calendar, awaiting the boys' return. My wife and I tried to amuse ourselves out of our newfound funk. We played many rounds of Let's See Who Can Go the Longest Without Talking About the Kids. Neither of us won. How did we live before we had kids? What did we talk about?

My wife reminded me that back then we spent an awful lot of time talking about *when* we would have kids, how *many* kids would we have, what it would be like to raise those kids . . . So even before they were here, we were talking about them. And now that they were gone, we were still talking about them.

"Didn't we ever talk about anything else?" I wondered.

"Once," my wife reminded me, "we talked about getting new plates."

I hadn't remembered. So apparently it wasn't that great a conversation.

WITH THE KIDS AWAY, the air in the house felt stale. Stagnant. The absence of chaos bordered on the creepy. There were no socks or quickly discarded basketball shorts draped over every other piece of furniture. Seeing toys neatly lined up on shelves instead of thrown all over the floor blocking any pedestrian passage now seemed simply *wrong.*

I remembered a friend sharing that the only time he ever lost his temper with his kids was when he stepped out of the shower and landed on a plastic yellow dinosaur, piercing his foot on the thing's tail. (In all fairness, it was a pterodactyl, which, in case you're not familiar, is known specifically for tail sharpness and rigidity. A brontosaurus tail, for example, would have likely been a non-issue.)

He continually harangued his kids about leaving toys lying about the floor. And now that his kids were out of the house and in college, he confessed to me, he regularly cursed the silence and the tidiness, and longed for nothing more than to once again step on a yellow dinosaur.

Now I knew what he was talking about; I was missing the dinosaurs. I tried tossing some toys and comic books willy-nilly around the floor, but it rang false; I wasn't kidding anybody. I couldn't match the authentic state of havoc my boys regularly produce with, literally, no effort.

I noticed that with the kids out of the house, even our dog was not himself. From the first moment he saw the duffel bags and sleeping bags come out, he knew something was up. I don't know if all dogs share this sensitivity to luggage, but our dog consistently falls into a pathetic melancholy whenever we so much as take down the suitcases. He instantly does the math: "Suitcase equals packing, packing equals leaving, and whoever those bathing suits and sunscreen are for, pretty sure it ain't me." What kills me, though, is the immediate and surprisingly mature resolve with which he accepts his impending abandonment. And, since dogs don't generally have a strong understanding of the calendar, they don't really know how long two weeks is. Or, for that matter, that there even is such a thing as a "week." As far as I can tell, dogs register only "here" and "not here." I would imagine they envision every departure to be the final one. Why would they assume anyone's ever coming back?

All the more impressive, then, that when he does see us pack to leave, our dog offers no significant protestations. No barking, like when he gets stuck in the garage. No whimpering, like when he wants your chicken. When he saw my boys pack for camp, there was just a slight cock of the head followed by a breathy, mournful sigh, bemoaning his inability to forestall the inevitable—not that different, come to think of it, from the sound my mother made when I went off to college. (Unlike my dog, however, I don't believe my mother then sank to the floor, laid her chin between her two extended arms, and stared at the bottom of the couch for nine hours. Though, again, I wasn't there to see, so . . . who knows?)

WITH HIS HUMAN BROTHERS out of the house, the dog definitely registered specific, tangible loss. There were far fewer belly rubs, far fewer playful romps and high-speed walks. There were half as many beds to share and half as many people who might potentially be shamed into dropping chicken.

My own sense of loss continued to reveal itself.

Flipping channels, for example, I realized that while I was now free to enjoy shows of my liking for far longer than I would normally, not having the boys there to persuade and convert made it less worthwhile. Stumbling across a Jerry Lewis/Dean Martin movie, for example, it was a refreshing treat to not have to fend off a chorus of "Uch, Daddy, it's black-and-white—it's so boring! Change it." But I also didn't have the challenge and sweet victory of getting them to love it.

As the days wore on, I began to realize that what I missed maybe more than anything was exactly that: my children's excitement.

From day one, your world is about trying to excite your children. You make funny noises to their face. You dangle red plastic keys over the crib for their amusement. Now, *you* know and *I* know the red key is not that great a toy; it's a piece of cheap plastic in the shape of a key. But *they* don't know that. They've never seen it before. It's fantastic. And *you* must be quite the aficionado for having such a thing in the first place, let alone the generosity of spirit to share it with them.

And childhood is an endless parade of more of the same. You point out the pretty truck, the picture of the clown, the cow in the field, the guy dressed up like Mickey Mouse . . . they love it all. And they love you for showing it to them. And you love it all because your children are happy, and you've helped facilitate that happiness. Everything is firing on all cylinders and life is grand. Until it's not.

There's a carnival near our house at the end of every summer. The kids love that carnival. They love the rides, the games, the noise, the once-a-year-ness of it, the tradition of it, the anticipation of it . . . everything.

A few months ago, we drove by the site, and with customary excitement, I pointed out, "Hey guys—two more months to the carnival!" There was a beat of silence, and then, just realizing it themselves, they both said, "You know what? I think I'm not really into the carnival anymore." My heart sunk. Obviously I didn't care about the carnival myself. I never even liked it. But I felt a crushing loss that it no longer excited *them*. (Never mind that now I had to come up with something new to dangle for their amusement.)

They had outgrown the carnival. As they should, I suppose. You wouldn't want your kid to still be fascinated with the shiny red plastic key when he's in high school. In time, almost everything will lose its appeal. In this case, my children had digested every-thing the carnival had to offer and, I'm guessing, come to see it for what it was: a dirty, dusty lot jammed tight with crappy rides oper-ated by toothless, joyless, vagabond carnies, moving, most likely, one step ahead of the law. Perhaps I overstate, but you get the point: it's just a lot of silly, noisy, artificial distraction. There's nothing really to it.

But let's be honest: there's nothing really to *anything*. When held up to the light, *nothing's* that terrific. Most of what we enjoy is enjoyable only because we declare it so. The real enjoyment is in the pointing out and the sharing. And that's what makes children in-dispensable: we need their excitement. Even when they *don't* like something, they dislike it with such gusto that everything is still better because of them. And we're the ones who reap the fruit. It's their enthusiasm we live off. It replenishes us. Rejuvenates us. Con-soles us. Without children, life just bounces back duller. Nobody likes a quiet carnival.

AS I LAY AWAKE at night, listening to the whir and hum of my house, staring at the glow of all the electronic twinkling and down-loading and charging, I charted my plan of action for the boys' re-turn: the second they come through that door, I resolved, I'm going to hug them until they can't breathe and then hug them a little more.

Not for them, mind you; for me. Entirely for me.

ACKNOWLEDGMENTS

MANY PEOPLE MUST BE THANKED FOR MAKING THIS BOOK a reality.

First of all, a big thank-you to Rob Weisbach—to whom I will be very careful what I say in the future. Apparently if you tell Rob you'd like to maybe, possibly, conceivably someday consider writing a book, it ends up there's a book.

An enormous, grateful, and heartfelt "where would I be without you" thank-you to my genius friend Jonathan Shapiro, he of the limitless talent and insight. It turns out it's a good thing we sit and talk about our kids—look what happens.

To Mr. Lenny Shapiro, whose enthusiasm for the first books encouraged the idea of doing this one.

To Ellen Archer, Elisabeth Dyssegaard, Gretchen Young, and all the fine people at Hyperion who made this too darn easy and pleasant.

To Peter Safran for keeping all the trains running.

To Peter Benedek, who sometimes has some darn good ideas, and who *always* operates with remarkable class and dignity.

To Katie Moeller for keeping track and remembering everything—all under a loudly ticking clock.

To my mother and father and sisters—not only for being such a great family but also because they let me talk about them in public like this and have never once—as of this writing—threatened legal action.

And, as ever, thank you thank you thank you to Paula, Ezra, and Leon for not only inspiring a book, but also being so understanding when I was so busy writing it. (Oh yeah—and also for making my life so magical and complete. That's very nice too.)